LEARN TO
FLY-FISH IN 24 HOURS

LEARN TO FLY-FISH IN 24 HOURS

An Hour-by-Hour Start-up Guide

Robert J. Sousa

Ragged Mountain Press/ McGraw-Hill

Camden, Maine ■ New York ■ Chicago ■ San Francisco ■ Lisbon ■ London ■ Madrid
Mexico City ■ Milan ■ New Delhi ■ San Juan ■ Seoul ■ Singapore ■ Sydney ■ Toronto

The McGraw·Hill Companies

1 2 3 4 5 6 7 8 9 DOC DOC 0 9 8 7 6

Library of Congress Cataloging-in-Publication Data
Sousa, Robert J.
  Learn to fly fish in 24 hours : an hour-by-hour start-up guide / Robert J. Sousa.
      p. cm.
  Includes index.
  ISBN-13: 978-0-07-147793-2 (pbk. : alk. paper)
  1. Fly fishing. I. Title.
  SH456.S625 2006
  799.12'4—dc22

                              2006017833

ISBN-13: 978-0-07-147793-2
ISBN-10: 0-07-147793-4

Questions regarding the content of this book should be addressed to
Ragged Mountain Press
P.O. Box 220
Camden, ME 04843
raggedmountainpress.com

Questions regarding the ordering of this book should be addressed to
The McGraw-Hill Companies
Customer Service Department
P.O. Box 547
Blacklick, OH 43004
Retail customers: 1-800-262-4729
Bookstores: 1-800-722-4726

Unless otherwise noted all photographs by the author.
Illustrations by Christopher Hoyt.

CONTENTS

AUTHOR'S INVITATION
Zen and the Art of Fly-Fishing

If you want to hear the grasshopper, you first must listen.

Out of the corner of your eye you think you see a flash. Immediately, with poetic balance, you float your fly gracefully on the wind to alight on the water near . . . Smash!

You have a fish on! What a glorious moment. You're awake, aware. You're connected with nature, perhaps for the first time since childhood.

Zen is awareness. It can be a religion and it can be a philosophy, but in essence it's an intuitive understanding having little to do with words and logic. To experience Zen awareness means to be awake to everything, to be free of distractions, to recognize that everything will change. Worry and agony are useless because they too will change.

Which is why fly-fishing provides an ideal path to Zen awareness. How else can we explain the attraction of this pastime? Everything I'm about to tell you is very Zen. You may even be Zen and not know it. Does it make any sense to spend thousands of dollars to catch a fish, only to release it unharmed? We might buy a boat, several fishing rods, a box full of lures, and who knows what other gear to fish on an occasional weekend, and the next week we go to the market and pay $6.98 a pound for the same fish we tossed back the previous Saturday.

How is it that someone with an IQ of 100+ can become so excited—hyper, really—in the pursuit and capture of an animal with an IQ of less than 2? What is the challenge in that? Why spend thousands of dollars to catch a fish? Are you insane?

No, you're Zen!

Since we both agree that we are not talking about logic here, let me relate something about the Zen of fly-fishing. In the movie *A River Runs through It*, Brad Pitt's character, Paul, admonishes never to be late for church, work, or fishing. In the scheme of things all three are important, yet if all can be melded into one, perhaps this is Zen. Clearly, the beautiful places you're likely to fish, the peaceful sound of moving water, and the bracing tonic of clean air all contribute to a healthier you. By their very nature, they set the stage for you to become Zen.

How can something as illogical as fly-fishing carry one from the depths of depression to the heights of emotional release? Is that even possible? Indeed it is. John Gierach, in his book *Fly Fishing the High Country,* closes by saying that rather than forgetting your troubles on a trout stream, what actually happens is you begin to see where your troubles fit into the grand scheme of things. In that overarching context, they're not such a big deal anymore.

What is it about fly-fishing that evokes feelings of peace, tranquility, and relaxation? Why do numerous TV commercials feature fly-fishing? I believe that fly-fishing has this effect because it's balanced. Everything about it enhances and is enhanced by balance. Nothing out of balance works; frustration builds, and the fish with its IQ of 2 gets away. But fly-fishing in balance is like poetry; it's as fluid as ballet or a concert in full harmony. It's beautiful to watch and even better to be doing.

So how do you learn these skills? How do you achieve this balance? Take another lesson from Zen: You must practice—not just the mechanical skills, but the mental skills as well. Patience, concentration, awareness, breathing . . . all in balance, all in harmony. The equipment does the work, but you're the conductor.

Perhaps best of all are the friendships you make while fly-fishing. You meet other Zenists, those also willing to spend big money to lure a fish to a fly. Those willing to travel near and far to see a fish rise to a fly. Those who will laugh and somehow understand your story of the one that got away. Those who also have allocated most or all of their brainpower to trick a fish to a fly. Those who forgo all logic to rediscover a childlike excitement and thrill they had long since forgotten.

A few years ago I met the tai chi master Chungliang Al Huang at a conference. Late one afternoon I was teaching fly tying, and at my invitation, he dropped by to see me. I tied him a small quill-bodied fly, to which he excitedly remarked, "Nature in miniature, nature in miniature." Later, after we discussed the calming effect of fly-fishing, he told me that I had found my *chi*. I don't claim to know exactly what he meant by chi, but fly-fishing opens a door to concentration, inner relaxation, and perspective. Tai chi is akin to fly-fishing in that it uses the graceful fluid movement and natural flexibility of the body to help you overcome the challenges of work and relieve stress, tension, and other sources of pain and discomfort. I can show you the path and teach you the fly-fishing skills, but the pursuit of balance and harmony is up to you.

The Zen of fly-fishing is about much more than catching a fish. Surely, as all sailors know, the journey matters more than the destination. The enjoyment is not in the catch but rather in tying a fly, presenting it to a fish with proper balance, and receiving that surge of adrenaline at the strike. Somehow, that moment puts your troubles in perspective. At the end of the day you have a story to tell. You have a friendship. You have a new life. You have found your chi. You're Zen!

HUR 1

LEARN ABOUT FLY-FISHING

I know with certainty that you can become a competent fly angler in 24 hours. While writing this book, I often pictured a young worker who has never fished before and for some crazy reason has just told his new boss that he is a fly angler. The response was, "Great, you must join me this weekend for some fly-fishing." Now he is really against the wall. How will he become competent in a sport he knows nothing about? Worse, how will he learn enough about fly angling before the weekend? This book solves that problem.

Fly-fishing is both easy and fun. Throughout this book you'll learn a commonsense approach and a few special tricks to help you on your way. My promise to you is that I'll make the learning process simple. Together we will disprove the myth that fly anglers must either be wealthy aristocrats with unlimited time and money or river rats who were born wearing waders. All you need is a good attitude, a dash of motivation, and a healthy supply of optimism. Fly anglers always believe that the glass is half full.

Your first questions might be, how do I start, what do I need, and how do I put all this stuff together? At this point you may not even know how to troll bait, let alone cast a fly rod. Don't worry. This book will carry you through an hour-by-hour progression of skills and information, with enough practice activities to make you a credible angler. Follow the instructions and you'll get there very quickly.

Not long ago I met a youngster while teaching fly-fishing at a National Boy Scout Jamboree. After I taught him how to cast, the scout asked me how much he'd have to pay for some good fly-fishing equipment. I knew that the Boy Scouts of America supply catalog listed an outfit for less than $100, and I told him about it, but he replied that he could hardly afford that kind of money. So I issued him a challenge. If he could complete all ten requirements for the Fly Fishing Merit Badge by the end of the day, I said, I would give him an outfit. "Now remember," I explained, "in addition to casting, you have to learn how to tie two flies and several knots; learn first aid and leave-no-trace practices; and catch two fish, one of which you must clean and cook." With that, the motivated boy disappeared, and when he showed up again at the end of the day he was smiling brilliantly. He proudly displayed a merit badge form indicating that he had completed all the requirements. I was thrilled. In one day he had gone from knowing nothing about fly-fishing to earning the badge, and he caught two fish. He walked away with a very good fly-fishing outfit and, I hope, a lifetime hobby.

We have to acknowledge that the scout had a few advantages, including going to established stations where he could get personalized instruction on each merit badge requirement. He also had before him a lake stocked with hungry fish, and he was handed balanced fly-fishing equipment that was rigged and ready to go. Since you'll be starting from the beginning, it might take a bit longer to reach the same level of competence—but not much longer.

Toward this end, the hourly schedule in this book will guide you through the process. Fly tying, a skill in itself, is mentioned last. If you're really against the time wall for your first trip out, you may wish to purchase a few flies to get you started, then begin tying them yourself later, as time permits.

The new employee I sometimes pictured while writing this book shares once crucial thing in common with the scout: motivation. They both want to learn, and they want to do it quickly. If you share this passion, your path to basic competency will be short, but please also recognize that one of the most intriguing elements of fly-fishing is that there is always something new to learn. Your level of knowledge and competency in this lifetime sport will continue to grow with each hour spent on the water.

Here is a preview of tips that we'll expand upon in later chapters.

▸ Get the right equipment for the fish you want to catch (Hours 2–5).
▸ Fish where the fish are likely to be (Hour 10).
▸ Once you're in the proper location, accurately deliver a fly that mimics what the fish may be eating (hours 8–9 and 11).
▸ Once you present the fly, quickly gain line control, set the hook, and be able to bring the fish to the net (Hours 12–13).

While all of this is simple, there are a few complexities that I'll help you through. Each of these steps, if you're to succeed, must be broken down to its essentials. In the following pages, I'll do just that.

This book assumes you know nothing of fly-fishing; indeed, that you have never fished before. This will actually make the task easier, as you will not be troubled with bad habits. I'll teach you how to cast, where to place the fly, how to set the hook, and how to land the fish. I'll recommend the kinds of equipment you might need and offer detailed suggestions on how to put it all together.

If you have any doubts about taking up this new sport, let me give you one more reason to try it. Each year, many people come to New England to see the fall colors. We call them "leaf peepers." I want to invite you to come to New England in mid-October, not only for the fantastic vistas of brilliant foliage, but also to witness the grandest and arguably the most beautiful fish of all, the native male brook trout in spawning colors. The whites, blacks, pinks, yellows, reds, browns, silvers, and more are resplendent, and they're on display for the lucky angler who catches one. Be advised, however, that this beauty will capture you forever!

Once Again, Why Is Fly-fishing So Special?

I keep coming back to this question because it can be answered in so many ways. One day a young Boy Scout wanted to fish, so he packed his rod and headed down to the river. As the day wore on, another angler asked him if he'd caught anything. He said no, he wasn't using a hook! All he had wanted to do, the boy told me later, was experience fishing. Catching fish to him was unimportant.

In Vietnam there are two seasons: hot and dry, and hot and wet. During the monsoon rains, there is water everywhere. On one exceedingly wet day in Vietnam, I decided to go fishing with a paper clip, a stick, and some string, which was all I had at the time. For me the object wasn't to catch fish but to go fishing.

Someone once asked the legendary Curt Gowdy, the voice of the Boston Red Sox during the 1960s and the noted host of the television program *American Sportsman*, why he so enjoyed fishing. Curt replied in a simple and most profound way, "I fish to please myself."

Clearly, fly-fishing attracts many people, and everyone seems to get something very different from it. As the complexity of everyday life increases, is it any wonder that more people are seeking the peaceful retreat of a gurgling brook or a tranquil lake? Here there is quiet, and the only crisis is which fly to use. Everything else is put aside as the fly fisher concentrates on making that delicate and perfect cast to a rising fish. As the fly line swings out gracefully behind in a beautiful tight loop, life isn't so bad after all. In essence, fly-fishing is a way to make things simple again. Whether you're an oldster, a youngster, or in between, catching a fish on a fly rod will evoke youthful exuberance. Fly-fishing is the key to eternal youth.

And what does fly-fishing have that other kinds of fishing don't? The answer is simple. Through some action on your part you provoke a fish to bite. Moreover, by using flies that closely mimic the size, shape, and color of what the fish are eating, we can catch more fish, and we enjoy more interaction with fish as we catch them, thanks to a fly rod's sensitive action. Certainly, fly fishing is a thoughtful and lifetime learning experience. As we invoke multiple strategies to entice a fish to take our fly, we become aware of many remarkable life forms and the intricacies of the natural world. Furthermore, catching fish with flies generally does not hurt the fish, which allows us to return them safely to the water.

Fly-fishing is not a passive sport that requires you to wait for something to happen. Rather, it's active; you must *make* something happen. By changing flies, changing location, fishing at a different depth, casting to a well-chosen spot, or using the right technique, you can provoke a fish into thinking your fly is a natural food that it wants to eat. This is the game, and like any other, it will take practice and effort to win. The challenge is finding the fish and then solving the daily puzzle of what the fish are eating. And the solution is different from one day to the next.

In a river about twenty minutes from my home, the water is clear, slow, and cold. One day, I noticed a nice rainbow trout there rising to take a morsel from the water's surface. I was about thirty feet downstream, and I made repeated casts, drifting my fly over this fish. I used every trick I knew and almost every fly in my box to entice it, but in 3 hours I failed to get even a nibble. All the while, the fish would rise every 5 to 10 minutes to take something minuscule from the surface. Finally, I waded ashore, put my fly rod on the riverbank, and went back into the river just below the fish. I studied that fish, watching him rise time and again. Anyone observing would have thought I was loony for sure. Perhaps they would have been right. Nonetheless, my patience was rewarded, as I watched that fish come up for a tiny insect and miss it. With great excitement, I positioned myself to await the bug now floating toward me. I think I captured it with as much excitement and pride as if I had caught the trout itself.

I quickly put my prize into my fly box and headed home. That very evening, I took it out and studied its size, color, and shape. It was extremely small, about the size of the smallest mosquito. I sat at my fly-tying table and made several flies that the fish might easily mistake for the real thing.

Daily work kept me away from that spot for about a week, but when I finally did get back, I saw the fish, "my fish," in almost the same spot it had been the week before. Sure enough, it was still periodically rising to take some small insect from the surface. Increasingly excited, I positioned myself about thirty feet downstream and fixed one of my new imitations to my tippet. I even used a high-tech 8X fluorocarbon leader (<2 lb. test), invisible underwater, to add further stealth. In my mind, I had already caught it.

Casting, I made a beautiful presentation and dropped the fly gently about four to five feet upstream from the fish. As my fly drifted gracefully and effortlessly down to it, I maintained great line control and got ready to strike by lifting my rod tip when it exploded on the fly. It was the perfect drift, the perfect fly; everything was right, but the fish, my fish, didn't budge. I kept on, cast after cast, but nothing. Meanwhile, the fish rose upon occasion for *something*, but it was not the fly I had imitated. It had changed its diet but never told me! The lesson for me is, while I think I'm good, there is always something to learn. I like to think that it doesn't happen often, but it does happen more than I care to admit. Fortunately, most fish are not as particular as this one was. If they were, there would be as many frustrated anglers on the river as there are lamenting golfers at a country club on a Saturday afternoon.

Yet another great thing about fly-fishing is its suitability for a family activity. At a Boy Scout Jamboree some years back, a young couple and their son stopped by to inquire about a low-cost fly rod package. While the father checked the fly rod out, the mother and son stood aside. I asked her if they wanted to learn how to cast a fly rod. Not wanting to inconvenience me, she declined, but I persisted, and since they were waiting anyway, they agreed. Somewhat reluctantly, the mother and son accompanied me a few yards to the waterfront, where I gave them a short lesson on how to cast. The mother listened intently, and from her first attempt she got it right, tight loops and all. She never made a bad cast. Then, I worked with her young son, and within a few more minutes, both of them were casting side by side in perfect symmetry. Excited at their progress, I ran up to get the father. As we rounded the corner and he saw them both casting beautifully, his jaw dropped. I put my arm around this fellow and told him that this was a present from me to him—a family activity they could do together. As we all walked back toward the rod racks, the mother asked me if anyone offered family fly-fishing vacations. I assured her that such things exist, and I could tell she was going to book one.

Ten Traits of a Good Angler

Here are the top ten traits that contribute to fly-fishing success. Once you begin to practice these, you'll be well on your way to becoming a competent angler.

1. Fish often.

During the season, I fish almost every day, and off-season, I have been known to fish during snowstorms while chipping ice from the line guides between casts. I'm retired now, but when I was working I carried my multipiece travel rod in my vehicle and would often stop to fish on my way home from the office. My goal was always to have a fish on a fly within 15 minutes of leaving the parking lot, and sometimes I did. At the beginning of the season, I occasionally met my boss at dawn to fish for an hour before heading into work. You can never be late for work if you fish with your boss!

Many fly fishers are on the banks or in the water during any kind of weather, including snowfall. Here, the author enjoys a bit of sunshine just after ice out.

One crisp October day I attended a meeting in a jacket and necktie. After the meeting I drove back to the office, arriving just after quitting time. Rather than go back to my desk and see if there was something I needed to attend to—note, there is always something on your desk that you need to attend to—I opted to head home. Arriving at the small pond near my house, I put on my chest waders, grabbed my fly rod, and started casting. After about a half hour, a photographer from a local newspaper showed up and started taking pictures, and when I was done fishing he asked for an interview. I answered his questions, but as he was about to leave, he turned with one more. "What's with the tie?" he asked. Only then did I realize that I had forgotten to take it off. "Don't you always wear a necktie when you go to church?" I asked in return, and we both laughed.

Fishing is always a highlight of my day. When you're concentrating on a fish, it's difficult to think about anything else. It's also an integral part of my daily exercise routine. Someone once said that a day of fishing does not count against the rest of your life. All fishing days are additive!

2. Be patient.

I'm not always patient in other aspects of my life, but I have been known to work a fish for several hours. Recently I landed one of the biggest trout (8.5 pounds and 28 inches) of my life after spending more than 5 hours casting to it. I actually have witnesses, tremendously patient people who were waiting for me while I made perhaps more than three hundred presentations to this fish. When I finally announced that I had it hooked, there were loud cheers and dances of glee. No doubt some of the jubilation was a release of frustration after waiting so long, but I like to think that there was a vicarious thrill at play, too, as when Tiger Woods sinks his final putt to win another Masters.

Nevertheless, with a big fish on, the onlookers wanted to net it right away. But I was using 6X (3 lb. test) tippet and a size 18 nymph (wicked small), so I held everyone at bay while waiting for the fish to show signs of fatigue. This took additional time, but when it comes to fishing, you must be very, very patient.

Once I locate where the fish are or where they're likely to be, I'm willing to plant my feet for several hours until I catch one (or more). If the fish are there, I'm perfectly content just to begin a process of picking them off one at a time. In these circumstances, I have two strategies. First, being a bit lazy, if I find a fly pattern that works, I'll continue to use it until it doesn't catch fish any longer. At that point, rather than move, I might start changing flies until I'm satisfied that I have caught most of the fish in the pool. My second strategy is to divide the pool into six sectors.

Fishing upstream, I'll cast to the downstream sector closest to me (1) and catch the available fish there. When I'm satisfied that I have done

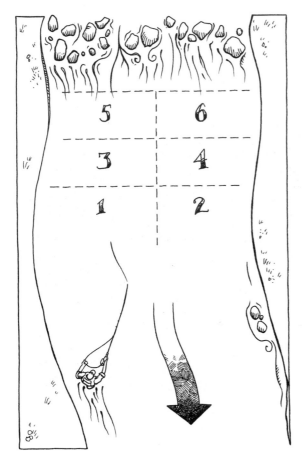

Hypothetical grid showing sectional fishing priorities. See text for description.

my best, I concentrate my casts to the opposite downstream sector (2). Then I cast upstream to the closer middle sector (3) and then to the more distant one (4), before finally casting to the upstream sectors (5, 6). This approach is not only methodical, it also avoids disturbing the upriver fish unnecessarily while I'm catching their downstream cousins. Fish are generally focused on what's happening upstream, as the current provides them their primary food source. While their attention is upstream, I catch fish after fish and use my fly rod pressure to lead each hooked fish downstream, where the battle will least likely impact or disturb the other feeding fish.

3. Look for fish where they're likely to be.

Over the years, I have figured out that fish are most likely to be just about where you expect them. Sure, there are exceptions, but for the most part they will hold in places where water currents bring them a steady supply of food and where they don't have to travel far to get it. Look for areas where one water current merges with another of a different speed, color, or turbidity (cloudiness). Also, you may find fish where the water is cooler or warmer than the main water mass. In early spring, the darker bottom

This angler is fishing where the water from two rivers mix. Notice the difference in color between the chalky main river (far side) and the clear tributary (near side).

shallows may hold more fish than the colder open water. In the dead of summer, fish may congregate just downstream from the confluence of a small, cold-water brook. Look for spring seeps, but be aware: fish in this shallow, clear water are going to be extremely skittish. They need to be in order to survive. Ospreys, eagles, and other fish-eating birds, as well as otters, like nothing more than to catch a nice fish dinner.

Look for areas where the current might cause food to collect; fish will be near. Lines of foam and bubbles on the water's surface will reveal the nuances of tricky currents and also carry insects in their flow. Fish sit beneath foam lines (and foam piles) and eat the insects as they float by. Foam lines are an excellent place to cast a fly. Back eddies are also good places to look for fish; however, because the current may be moving in the opposite direction, presenting a good, drag-free drift can be a challenge.

A calm, quiet backwater with lots of overhead cover will sometimes hold big trout, so use stealth and approach the fish very carefully.

Fish also like overhead protection, so look for them under trees, cut banks, and other places most people can't or won't cast to. I like to check just downstream of a riffle, where the water deepens and flattens out. Usually these areas are well oxygenated, and fish holding there get first dibs on any food coming off the riffle. The tail of a pool is another place to find fish. Check out the water just above where the water increases speed and perhaps starts another riffle. Always thoroughly check out any location where the channel moves from one side of the river to the other. Target the area beside but not necessarily *in* the faster moving water of the channel. These seams often hold feeding fish. Also look for *pocket water*—quieter water in these spots where a fish might hold—on the downstream sides of rocks or logs. (I'll talk more about fish habitat and where to find fish in Hour 10.)

Always be alert for a rising fish. Good, bronze-tinted polarized glasses can help you see signs of fish that someone less equipped won't see. Sometimes when I'm drifting a fly, I might see a slight flash or something different. These often-subtle signs may represent a fish. I'll always work these areas with multiple casts in the hope that perhaps a fish will honor me with a strike.

4. Always try to improve.

Every seasoned angler has unique knowledge, experience, and plenty of tricks that seem to be second nature. I like to fish with these folks, as I often notice subtle things they do that allow them to catch a fish where most anglers can't. Watching these masters is like watching a great surgeon or violin maker. It's like listening to a gifted musician play a vintage Martin guitar—you wonder where and how the beautiful notes were made. They know their craft, and they set about making that fly rod an instrument of skill and beauty. Like Babe Ruth predicting a home run, they can sometimes even call the particular cast that will catch a fish. When you come upon an angler like this, watch closely and try to learn the skills he or she is demonstrating, then add them to your tackle box.

If someone develops a new technique, give it a try. See if it works for you. Fishing is a lifetime experiment; some ideas will work and others won't. The only constant is nature itself. Along the way you'll have great fun, meet wonderful people, visit marvelous locations, and enjoy life.

When you're fishing with someone who obviously knows more about fly-fishing than you, ask questions about their favorite flies and the techniques they have developed. While some anglers might not talk a lot on the water, they can be a wealth of information before or after the fishing day. Really pick their brains. Your questions and enthusiasm are often all they need to begin a flow of suggestions and an exchange of ideas. Also, if you actually do find yourself facing a day of fishing with your boss or someone to whom you would rather not show how green you are to the sport, feel free to ask questions. Where will we be going? What are your favorite flies for this place? What size flies do you recommend? What are the license requirements? (All states require a license in freshwater fishing and many also require a license for saltwater fishing.) What size rod will you be using? What equipment should I bring? Do I need any specialized items? What fish will we likely catch? Each of these questions is reasonable and should not give your greenness away. Moreover, the answers will help you form a strategy for how to proceed. Be sure to take notes during the conversation. Fly anglers always take notes!

5. Be flexible.

Don't restrict yourself to catching only one kind of fish. If the trout aren't biting, but the smallmouth bass are, enjoy catching smallmouth. Other species like bluegill, crappie, fallfish, perch, rock bass, and largemouth bass are great fun on a fly. Some of my friends even try to catch carp on

That's worth a merit badge. This young angler proudly shows a pond shiner caught on a fly.

mulberry fly imitations. Also, when your freshwater fishing haunts get too warm in mid-summer, go fishing in salt water.

Once you get the hang of fly-fishing, you may find that you're ready to try new waters instead of going to the same place to fish every day. Fishing the same waters can become quite boring. Instead of becoming a specialist on one river or fishery I strive to be competent on them all. Moving around allows me to perfect a variety of techniques, all of which help me become a complete angler. Fortunately, I live in an area where I can fish in four quality rivers all within about twenty or thirty minutes from my home. We also have a wealth of ponds, lakes, and smaller streams that have healthy fish populations. In addition, within two hours I can be salt-water fishing. If you're blessed with such variety of fishing spots and fish, or even just two or three, I encourage you to try them all. Enjoy the diversity of fishing in different places.

6. Be focused.

Fishing is like any other hobby you find worthwhile: you practice, then practice some more until you have honed your skill. By concentrating in such a way, you do get better, and better leads to good, and good to great. After a game, Ted Williams, the last best batter in baseball and the only major league player to hit over .400 in a single season, would stand in front of a mirror and in his mind revisit every pitch he saw that day. He was focused! That may be big-league intensity, but to become skilled at fly-fishing, you need a high degree of focus.

7. Turn weakness into strength.

I'm nearsighted, yet I've turned this weakness into a strength. You might ask, How can such a flaw in vision possibly become a fly fisher's strength? Try tying a size 28 hook with 8X tippet and you'll immediately see the advantage of being nearsighted. I may have to take off my glasses to see these fine dimensions, but when I do the Lilliputian world of micros is in my grasp. By being able to see and work with the small stuff I can give even those really big fish—who sometimes limit their food to really small things—what they want, and I become a better angler because of it. Fly fishers have been known to adapt their casting methods to bypass physical limitations, and right-handed fishers have become proficient at casting with their left hand when a situation calls for it. The message here is don't give in to your weaknesses.

Some folks consider knowing nothing at all about fishing to be a weakness when learning to fly-fish. This is not so. Since you don't have the mindset or bad habits of a lure angler, all you need to do is learn the simple casting techniques taught in this book. Unlike traditional lure or bait fishing, in which the sheer weight of the lure helps the cast, fly-fishing uses the weight of the fly line to propel and deliver the fly to the fish. Flies generally don't weigh much, and you don't have to strong-arm the fly rod to present your fly properly. Casting a fly is more a function of timing than arm strength.

8. Improve dexterity.

Once when I was young I tore a shirt, and my mother encouraged me to repair it myself. Hand sewing—and I'm not talking seamstress quality here—was an early skill I picked up, mainly through trial and error. Working with thread and fine tolerances will allow you to tie flies on size 28 hooks (really small). It will also help you when you get into trouble. For example, a fly rod is a knot-tying machine: the more you wiggle the tip, the more likely the fly line and leader will tie themselves into all sorts of Gordian-like contrivances. At times like this it doesn't pay to get angry; instead, just sit down and untangle the mess. Whether you're untangling fly line or tying the tiniest

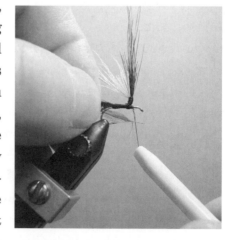

It takes nimble fingers and some dexterity to tie flies like this Black Gnat Parachute.

of flies, if you begin with an I-can-do-this attitude you'll soon learn that, by golly, you can!

9. Become an accurate caster.

Sure, this will take practice, but I highly recommend putting more effort into developing accuracy skills than trying to cast longer distances. Accuracy allows you to put a fly where another angler can't. Occasionally these difficult-to-hit spots may hold that trophy fish.

With considerable practice, I have become a fairly accurate caster, so I'm not afraid to cast within inches of a debris pile or a bank dense with brush. This doesn't mean that my cast is always perfect, but fortunately for me, a miss doesn't happen that often.

Once you get your gear together, lay a few paper plates on the lawn and practice casting to them. *Wherever you practice, be sure to stand away from overhead wires, trees, and people.* Instead of a fly, tie a small piece of colorful yarn to the end of 5 feet of 8 lb. test monofilament fishing line. Note that a tapered leader is expensive, so you don't want to use one for this type of practice; the short piece of monofilament will work just fine.

You might also go to a neighborhood pond and, like a golfer practicing on a putting green, make cast after cast to some imaginary target. As your accuracy improves, keep moving the target around or make it smaller. Vary your distance. You know you have arrived when you can consistently cast your fly to some floating object, like a leaf, thirty feet away. Remember, the only way to maintain this accuracy is to practice on a regular basis. (I'll talk more about casting in hours 8–9 and 17.)

10. Make lots of friends.

My father always says it's better to make a friend than a dollar. Using that principle I have never sold a fly, but I've given away literally thousands. Each fly takes time to tie, so when I give one away I'm giving away some of my most precious asset: time. Once when my son and I were returning from a fishing trip, we stopped for gas. While we were inside paying, the vehicle—and the chest pack containing all of my flies and accessories—was unattended, and within 5 minutes someone purloined the pack along with the four or five hundred flies contained therein. At a rate of about 10 minutes tying time per fly it would have taken me scores of hours to replace them all.

When a friend heard about my plight, he sent me a whole box of flies. This generosity was totally unexpected, but it's quite typical of the fly-fishing community. As a group we love our sport, and we are very protective of the resources on which it depends. Together, each fly angler becomes part of a fraternity. We care about each other and we care about the new people coming into the sport. We also care about the quality angling experiences we hope to enjoy. Natural beauty and productive fish habitat are often inexorably linked. As a fly angler, you'll make new friends. You'll lament to a sympathetic ear about the big one that got away. And at the end of the day you'll smile, laugh and be as content as you possibly can be, because by using stealth and guile and maybe even a fly you tied yourself, you caught a fish and can now tell your new friends all about the experience!

One Last Bit of Advice

When it comes to any aspect of fly-fishing—whether tying a fly, casting it, or fighting a big fish—know that it's OK to think for yourself. You don't always have to conform to what others are doing. Allow your creativity and cleverness to shine when the opportunity presents itself. A few years ago I was invited to tie flies at a fly-fishing show in Rhode Island. Many other tiers were there, and they were all tying large saltwater flies. I decided to go to the absolute other extreme and tie micro flies. Not only did I add diversity to the show, I convinced many anglers that tying tiny flies is, in fact, possible.

The lesson here is, when you see everyone else going in one direction, try going the other way. Doing something different may test new skills and ultimately enhance self-confidence. Further, you may actually discover something new and innovative to advance the sport. Mostly, however, you will have fun.

While most everyone else was home in bed, this crafty angler did something different: he went fishing! To catch big fish, you sometimes you have to fish at night when they're more vulnerable.

Time Check

You might be finishing this chapter with a mixture of delight and dismay—delight because you've used only a portion of your first hour (you might be thinking, "At this rate, I'll be a fly fisher in 12 hours, not 24!"), dismay because you haven't yet learned how to cast or tie a knot. But don't worry; you've learned something far more important. You've learned to think like an angler while maintaining an optimistic and motivated attitude, and that will make the rest fun and almost effortless.

HURS 2–5

FLY TACKLE AND OTHER EQUIPMENT

Before you can catch fish, you'll need something to catch them with. As with golf, there is a wonderful array of equipment from which to select. Do you need all of it? Of course not. My goal is to lay out the essentials and let you go from there. As you develop your skills, your need for gear will increase accordingly.

Before we get into specifics, let me offer a few general tips. You might be tempted to borrow equipment from a friend or to use gear that was given to you a while back. You may even have picked up an old rod at a yard sale, thinking you might try the sport one day. The problem with this equipment is it represents an unknown. While it may very well be good, you just don't know. What you need is a balanced outfit for the type of fishing you'll be doing. For example, a light freshwater rod and reel will not do you much good for most saltwater fish.

How can you determine whether what you have will work? If you have a friend who is an avid fly fisher, you might ask for help in evaluating your equipment. Another idea is to take your gear to a local fly shop and have someone who really knows fly-fishing look at what you have. Without doubt, a local shop can be your best source of equipment evaluation as well as valuable information on local fishing. If the staff there don't know, they usually know someone who does. Local shops are in business because they offer service you just can't get at the big box stores like Wal-Mart or Target. If you have a fly shop in your area, treasure it and become a frequent customer.

Other sources of advice include the local chapter of Federation of Fly Fishers or Trout Unlimited. Local contacts for both organizations can often be found through a Web search. Again, you'll generally find these people to be open and receptive. Avoid showing up for your first day on the stream with untested equipment. While you may luck out, you run a high risk of a less-than-satisfactory experience. You certainly do not want your day to be spoiled because of equipment failures. So, if you have older equipment, at the very least have someone who really knows the sport give you some advice beforehand; it may just save your day.

For our purposes here, I'll assume that you have no fly-fishing gear and need to obtain some. Following are some key tips on what to look for and how you can evaluate what items will work best for the fishing you'll be doing. Let the accompanying table serve as a quick guide. You may want to adapt these recommendations to special preferences or circumstances, but they will get you into the ballpark. And four hours should be ample to decide on a start-up equipment kit and to obtain your tackle and gear—even if your shopping trip mires you in crosstown traffic!

In fly-fishing, the objective is to deliver the fly to the fish's vicinity and make it believe that your fly is something it wants to eat. Sheer trickery! If the fly is indeed to arrive accurately in front of the fish, each component— rod, reel, backing, fly line, leader, tippet, and fly—needs to be carefully integrated. As in a train, if everything is not linked and balanced, problems may occur and components will go astray.

As described in the table, the rod size is dictated by the size fish you may be seeking, the size and bulk of the fly you'll be casting, and the depth

Choose Gear Suited to the Size of the Fish

FISH LENGTH	ROD WEIGHT	LINE WEIGHT	TAPER	BACKING TEST	FLY SIZES	NOTES
<10″	1	1–2	weight-forward floating	10	28–12	soft, delicate presentations
	2	2–3				
	3	3–4				
10–20″	4	4–5	weight-forward floating, sinking, and sink tip	20	28–4	most freshwater applications
	5	5–6				
	6	6–7				
20–30″	7	7–8	weight-forward floating, sinking, and sink tip	20–30	14–2	larger freshwater and general coastal saltwater fish
	8	8–9				
	9	9–10				
30–40″	10	10–11	weight-forward floating, sinking, and sink tip	30	2–6/0	larger salmon and bluewater big-game species
	11	11–12				
	12	12–13				
>50″	13	13–14	weight-forward floating, sinking, and sink tip	40–50	large custom-tied flies	large bluewater game fish, sailfish, tuna, and marlin
	14	14–15				
	15	15				

of water you'll wish your fly to fish. Generally speaking, lighter-weight rods are designed to catch smaller fish, and heavier rods—because of their increased stiffness—can cast larger flies and more effectively land larger fish. I do not advocate targeting large fish on light fly rods because of the additional stress imposed on fish during extended battles.

Fly Line

With the above points in mind, the key component of the fly delivery system is the fly line. If you understand how fly lines are constructed, weighted, and tapered, you'll better understand which rod weight best suits the fish you want to catch. It follows, then, that we should begin our discussion of equipment with the fly line. If you get the correct fly line, everything else will follow nicely.

In general, floating lines are used to fish flies at or near the surface. Sinking tip lines work well at depths to about eight feet; when fishing deeper water, use full sink lines.

Lots of good fly lines are being made today, and they have all sorts of proprietary coatings that reduce friction as the line moves through the rod guides, enabling your casts to travel farther with minimal effort. I find today's lines a quantum improvement over what my grandfather gave me when I was starting out fifty years ago.

A key point to remember is that it's the weight of the fly line, and particularly the extra weight added in the first thirty feet, that casts the fly. This is quite different from lure fishing, in which it's the lure that has the weight and the line is essentially weightless. The weight of a fly is much less than that of a typical jig, spoon, or fishing plug, so it's the controlled unrolling of the line that allows you to deliver the fly to the fish.

To select a fly line, you must first consider the taper and weight of the line. Next, determine whether you need a line that floats, partially floats, or fully sinks; its sink rate; and then perhaps its color.

By industry convention, every fly line is denoted by a series of letters and numbers. For example, WF6F means Weight-Forward 6 Floating, in which the number "6" is the weight. You'll need to know what these designations mean and how each will affect your casting. The following taper designations are standard:

WF = Weight-Forward
DT = Double Taper
ST = Shooting Taper, or Shooting Head
TT = Triangle Taper
L = Level Taper

Fly line taper is critical to how a cast is made and how your fly unrolls toward the fish. Each taper has its use, but don't waste your money on a level-tapered fly line. Level tapers are inexpensive, but as far as I'm concerned they're worthless. Except for trolling—which isn't really fly-fishing—I can't think of a good use for level lines. Even expert casters avoid them.

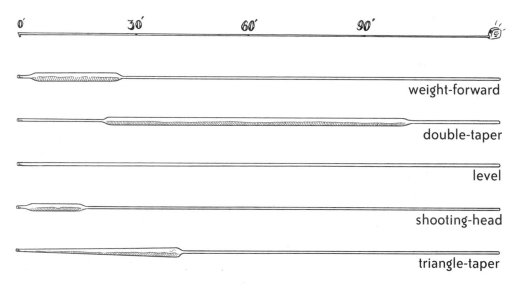

For the best overall taper, choose a fly line that's weight-forward. Triangle-taper fly line is one of the best unfurling fly lines, while double taper line is the best bargain. Note, too, that double-taper line can be reversed when one end becomes worn. When you need to make long casts, use shooting-head line. Avoid using level line unless you plan to do some trolling.

The weight numbers that comprise the second portion of a fly line code designation pertain to the added grain weight in the first thirty feet, with one grain equaling 0.0648 gram or 0.002 ounce. Here's how it breaks out.

Fly line weight	Number of grains
1	60
2	80
3	100
4	120
5	140
6	160
7	185
8	210
9	240
10	280

11	330
12	380
13	440
14	500
15	550

The last letters in the fly line code relate to the use of the fly line as follows:

F = Floating
S = Sinking
S/T = Sinking Tip

Use floating lines to cast dry flies (flies that float) or wet flies (flies that sink) in shallow water. Use sinking lines when you want to get your wet fly down to a specific depth. You generally would use a sinking-tip line in shallower water when you want your fly to sink, but not so far that it creates extra work to lift the line out of the water for the next cast. Since part of the line floats, lifting a sinking-tip line off and out of the water is a bit easier.

Beyond these standard codes, manufacturers have developed all sorts of specialty lines for one purpose or another. For example, there are lines with clear tips and interchangeable tips and lines with variable sink rates. The Triangle Taper offered exclusively by Royal Wulff features a continuous taper in the front part of the fly line that gives an efficient transfer of energy as the line unrolls. Fly line manufacturing and marketing has become a science unto itself, and about the only additional innovation I'd like to see is a fly line that doesn't have any coil memory. I'm sure someone will do it, but I have yet to find the perfect one.

If I had but one fly line for freshwater applications, it would be a reel filled with a Weight-Forward 6 Floating (WF6F) fly line. (So, you see, my choice of an example above wasn't entirely random.) On a second reel or spool, I might carry a Weight-Forward 6 Sinking Tip (WF6S/T) line. These lines give me the option to fish on the surface or at depth merely by changing spools. When I know I won't be moving much, I carry two rods already strung and don't even have to take the extra time to change the spools. Leaving one rod on the bank, I merely switch back and forth as the fish rise or as whim dictates.

For saltwater fishing, I use a WF8F line for fishing in shallow water—say, on a bonefish flat—or a WF8S/T line if I plan to fish water a bit deeper.

Good fly line costs a bit more today than it did when I was younger, but if you shop around you can sometimes find great lines for very reasonable prices. When shopping online, look for the occasional closeouts at www.sierratradingpost.com. If you do find bargain lines, however, be sure they're not so old that the plastic coating has started to break down. You may even find small cracks that indicate they're brittle. Obviously, if you get any of these, return them at once. For additional information on fly lines and their tapers, refer to www.rioproducts.com.

One last tip about fly lines before we move on: when I go on a long trip I bring along a few extra fly lines just in case. For example, I might carry two WF6F and two WF8F lines, as well as sinking-tip lines in 6 and 8 weights. All this redundancy provides added flexibility to replace a severely damaged fly line dragged across sharp rocks by an extremely angry fish. Sometimes, small extras like these can save the day for you or one of your fishing companions.

Fly Rod

Now that you understand the concept of line weight, the transition to fly rod weights is an easy one. Rod manufacturers help us by designating their rod weights to perform best with fly lines of a similar weight designation. Since your goal is to build a balanced outfit, simply match the weight of the rod to the weight of the line. It's important to note, however, that lower weights are generally used to catch smaller fish. For most freshwater applications I like a 5- or 6-weight (wt) rod matched with comparably sized fly line. In salt water, I generally use 8- or 9-weight rods matched with a similar weight line. Sometimes I use a fly line that's one weight

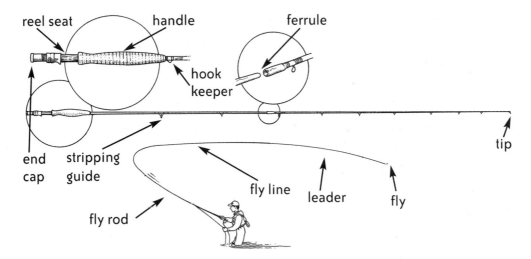

Fly rod anatomy.

class heavier than the rod designation to help propel larger or heavier flies. Using a slightly heavier line can also help a beginning caster feel the casting action of the rod more successfully.

This brings us to *fly rod action*. Fly rods have soft, medium, or fast actions. A soft rod has a lot of flex, and when a cast is made with a soft- or slow-action rod, it takes a bit longer to transfer energy from the rod to the line.

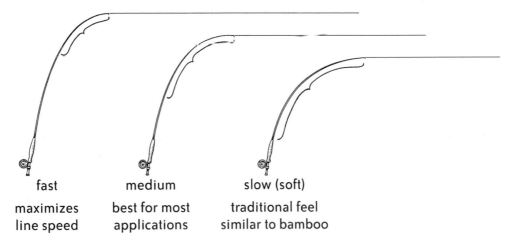

Fast-action fly rods express the most flex in the tip. Medium- and slow- or soft-action fly rods express more flex in their lengths, with soft-action rods having the greatest length of flexibility.

A medium-action rod transfers this energy a bit faster, while a fast-action rod requires more energy to get it to flex, but releases that energy quickly to the line in the casting sequence, increasing both line speed and casting distance.

When I was a bit younger, I loved fast-action, high-modulus graphite rods. The more millions of modulus (a manufacturers' designation) a rod advertised, the better I liked it. It seemed to me that I could impart a lot of energy into high-modulus rods, and when that energy was unloaded, the fly line would zing out there. But I'm not so hot on high-modulus rods these days, in large part because, as I get older, the ligaments in my arm and especially in my elbow are becoming increasingly inelastic. The vibration caused by the flexing and unflexing of a high-modulus rod tip has to go somewhere, and as these waves of energy travel down the rod they pass through the rod handle and into my thumb, hand, forearm, and finally the epicondyle ligament in my elbow. With repeated casts, a painful condition similar to tennis elbow results.

As a result of this "angler's elbow," I'm not recommending you purchase a fast-action fly rod, at least not initially. If you want to get one later, be my guest, but for your first rod, I suggest one with a medium-flex action. A medium-action rod is suitable to a wide range of casting styles and circumstances and should load easily. (I will discuss load in detail later, with casting.) Moreover, you'll better feel the loading of the rod on your backcast, letting you know when to begin moving the rod forward. There are many medium-action rods out there, and it should not be difficult to find just the right one for you. The rod with the most well-known brand name may not necessarily be any better than one that costs much less. Rod manufacturers are constantly making improvements, and competition is forcing down prices on really good equipment.

There seems to be a fly rod for just about everyone and every circumstance. Some are built for travel and break down into multiple pieces, but most have only two sections. To assemble the rod, the tip of one section is inserted into the butt end of the other at the interlocking ferrule joint. A slight twist to seat and align them secures them in place.

Most fly rods are between 8 and 9 feet long. For the most part, they need to be this long in order to keep 30 or more feet of fly line in the air during casting. In windy conditions, some anglers use rods that are 10 feet long or longer to get the line that much higher above the water. At the more specialized end of things, there is recent interest in two-handed Spey casting with 12- to 18-foot rods, allowing anglers to make long presentations using a modified roll cast. But again, for your purposes, a rod between 8 and 9 feet long will work just fine.

One quick way to determine whether a fly rod is any good is to watch the tip recover (stop moving up and down) when you stop shaking it. A tip that continues to quiver after shaking is not necessarily a good thing, as each time it does so it imparts added friction on the fly line. Cumulatively, these waves of resistance from a vibrating rod tip act as a brake, reducing the distance of your cast. What you're looking for is a relatively fast recovery, and a too soft tip doesn't fit that requirement.

One of the best places to look for a fly rod is your local fly tackle shop. These folks specialize in giving quality service—the best way to compete with the big box stores—so they should be able to give you the time you need to make the right decision. Another place to compare rods is at any of the outdoor or fishing shows that come to your area. Here you can try the rods of many manufacturers, ask questions of the experts, and select the perfect match.

Travel Rods versus Two-Piece Rods

I should say a word about multipiece travel rods versus two-piece rods. Two-piece rods are probably better when fishing within driving distance of your home, but they become a big constraint for air travel. When I travel, I always want to be sure my essential fly-fishing gear will arrive with me at my fishing destination, so I hate to check it. Yet carrying the long, two-piece rod tubes in an overhead compartment is a privilege of the past. Nowadays airlines will allow you one carry-on bag and one other small personal item. Since I want to carry on my waders, flies, reels, and rods along with some clothing, a fifty-inch rod tube or two is out of the question. Instead, I can carry two multipiece travel rods nested on either side of my day pack.

On a typical trip, I often pack two additional multipiece rods inside my roll-on suitcase or small backpack, giving me four travel rods altogether in the following weights: 5-weight, 6-weight, 8-weight, and 9-weight. The 6-weight rod can serve as a backup to the 5-weight, and the 8-weight backs up the 9-weight. These rods allow me to go from small to larger fish or from fresh- to saltwater fishing very easily. Furthermore, as the poet Robert Service suggests, strange things happen under the midnight sun, and once in a while you'll accidentally break a rod. My solution when I'm way out there is to carry spares. Backups can save an expensive fishing trip.

So how do these multipiece rods function? I notice little difference in the actions of two-piece and modern multipiece rods. Yes, you have to check the alignments of the guides along multiple sections, but if the rod has alignment dots, this is easy. As in all rods, you should also check the tightness of the ferrule connections between sections every once in a while, but again this should be standard practice. Even close to home, I'll carry an extra travel rod with me as a spare. I learned this lesson some years ago when I was out fishing and accidentally broke my rod. This bit of misfortune killed my fishing day, as I had no quick access to a spare rod. With the cost of travel rods quite reasonable and their performance virtually indistinguishable from two-piece rods, there is no reason not to own at least one such rod.

There are some great travel rods on the market today, and some companies offer no-excuse lifetime guarantees against breakage.

A couple of true anecdotes will drive home the point about carrying your essential gear with you on the plane. Some years ago, I went with a friend to Alaska to fish. My buddy opted to check his gear, but I carried mine on board, as I always do. In Anchorage we were to switch to a small plane into the bush, but at the baggage area we learned that his bag was sent on to Japan, and it would not make it back to Anchorage for several days. While most of the loss was insured, we had to delay our flight and scramble around to find and buy replacement gear. This caused a lot of aggravation and a significant loss in fishing time.

Another time I was traveling to an outdoor writers' conference near Jackson Hole, Wyoming. My traveling companion and I missed a connection at the Denver airport and had to be rerouted through Salt Lake City. You guessed it: our baggage did not arrive at our final destination, but because I had carried my fishing gear aboard, I was at least able to fish. It was Saturday evening and all the stores were closed, so we headed to the conference center about twenty miles out of town.

The mix up may have left me without clean clothes, but I still had my fishing gear. The next afternoon we set out to go fishing.

As we stood overlooking the river, my buddy suggested that I cross to the other side so we both could fish within a short distance of each other. I agreed and began crossing. About halfway across, however, the current swept my legs out, and downstream I went. I was in no danger, but I got good and wet before I could reach dry ground. So, I took the opportunity to wash my only clothes streamside. Now I at least had clean clothes for the meeting. Long story short: if fishing is a priority, your fishing gear must stay in your control. Clothing can be borrowed, purchased, or at least washed, but fishing gear is fishing gear.

Fly Reel

A fly reel has been described as a device on which you store fly line, but I think it's much more than that. Sure, you can put your fly line neatly onto the spool, but you can also add fly line backing (see below), enabling you to fight and land the big one after it makes its first challenging run of 150 feet or more. The backing's volume (i.e., its thickness) also will help you to recover your fly line more quickly. Since you can only crank the reel handle so fast, a spool packed with backing will reduce the number of cranks—this is especially helpful if you have a big fish on. The other feature a reel should have is a drag. Engineers build friction systems into their reels to add resistance when fly line is being pulled from the reel. The best reels have adjustable drag systems, which apply even pressure

Palming complements the drag action of a fly reel, and is an especially handy technique to know if you have a cheaper reel.

on the line as a fish makes a run away from you.

Cheaper reels have less effective drag systems. These reels can, however, be supplemented by a technique called *palming*. Palming is when you use the palm of your free hand to add braking pressure to the rim of the reel. The added friction complements the reel's drag and is particularly helpful when you can't easily increase the reel's drag setting. For more resistance, increase the pressure your palm exerts on the rim. This technique works on almost any reel in which the outside rim of the spool is exposed.

TIP: Don't try to slow down a runaway fish by holding the reel handle. This is a great way to break the handle, break a finger, or otherwise severely bruise your hand. When big fish take off, they go with a lot of power, and reel drags have been known to smoke, literally. When the reel handle is spinning rapidly, keep your hand away.

As reels become more sophisticated and costly, so do their drag systems. I have a 5th reel with a turbine drag system in which a small turbine spins in a sealed oil bath. The faster the spin, the more drag is generated by the resistance of the oil.

For the most part, when it comes to reels, you get what you pay for. There are some well-engineered reels made of high-quality bar stock aluminum that have great drag systems. Each of these reels has to be machined separately and is, accordingly, expensive. In essence, you want a drag that pulls smoothly and with the same tension from the initial pull until the fish stops running.

Fortunately, for someone who just wants a competent reel but doesn't want to spend $200 or more, I can recommend the venerable Pflueger Medalist. This reel has been around for a long time, and its cost is still quite reasonable. For simple freshwater applications, I like Models 1494 and 1495. You should be able to find these reels just about anywhere—including your local fly shop and Wal-Mart—for about $30 or less. Given its capabilities, this is just a great little reel and a great bargain. You may also be able to find them used. I know people who use the Model 1498 for saltwater applications, and they swear by it. My guess is that since these reels were not made for the corrosive potential of seawater, their owners must have to take extra care in lubrication and cleaning after each use. This reel is not a great reel, but it's very good, and for the price, you may want to get two, using the second for your backup fly line.

Backing

Fly line backing is generally a strong (usually about 20 or 30 lb. test) low-stretch braided polyester (i.e., Dacron) fishing line. Its length is usually about one hundred yards or more with the end tied onto the arbor of the reel's spool. Besides filling the spool to help lessen those tight memory coils in your fly line, the primary purpose of backing is to allow a fish to make a long run away from you. Sometimes these runs will exceed the length of the fly line, and then the only attachment you have to your $60 fly line is the nail knot (see Hours 6–7, Tying Knots and Assembling the Fly-Fishing Tackle) you tied to your backing. Now is not the time to question that knot! At any rate, you'll always be relieved when after reeling like crazy you recover a few cranks of fly line onto the reel. Again, due to the bulk created by the backing, you won't have to crank as many turns to get your fly line back onto the spool.

If you're going after bigger fish, you may wish to put 30 lb. test backing line on the reels for the 8- and 9-weight fly lines. Similarly, 20 lb. test backing is usually adequate for 5- and 6-weight fly line applications. Higher rated backing may be needed for even larger fish.

TIP: Do not be tempted to use SpiderWire or similar fishing line as backing. This line is great for its intended purpose, but when under tension it can cut right through your nail knot, and there goes your $60 fly line.

Leader and Tippet

A *leader* is a tapered length of monofilament or braided line that's used to present the fly to the fish. The taper, heavier at the butt and finer where the fly is tied, allows the line to roll out easily and gently as the cast is completed.

Because the fine tapered end of the leader is gradually cut away during repeated fly changes, it eventually becomes necessary to replace what's been lost. A *tippet* serves this function. A tippet is often a 24-inch length of monofilament fishing line. It is added to the terminal end of the leader to restore its original length.

Being lazy, I do not tie my own tapered leaders any longer. I just use the prepackaged leader that comes direct from the factory. You can buy them in just about any line strength you need. At the heavier butt section, I tie a double surgeon's loop and make a loop-to-loop connection with the fly line (see Hours 6–7, Tying Knots and Assembling the Fly-Fishing Tackle). Scientific Angler recently introduced a new product called L2L (for line to leader) that makes this connection literally a snap. I have used this easy connector system and it works quite well.

For the past several years I have been using Seaguar fluorocarbon tippet and leaders. This is excellent quality material, but it also can be a bit expensive. The big advantage of fluorocarbon is that it has about the same refractivity index as water, so the leader becomes virtually indistinguishable when it's underwater. If the fish can't see it, they won't be alerted to some unnatural line attached to your fly. This is a big advantage when fishing still or very slow clear water where the fish have a lot of time to really scrutinize the fly before deciding whether or not to eat it.

TIP: After casting your dry fly, a few inches of tippet may rest on top of the water, creating an unnatural look to your fly. Often a quick, short strip or two (i.e., one or two tugs on the fly line) at the beginning of the float will draw the tippet underwater, leaving only the fly on the surface. Another technique is to rub the last ten inches of your tippet with a special liquid, such as Zink, which is designed to eliminate surface tension, thus allowing the end of the tippet to sink.

When you're not sure which tippet size to use, follow the rule of 3: divide the hook size by 3 to estimate the tippet size. For example, if you use a size 12 hook, you would use a size 4 tippet (12/3 = 4). In general, I like to use 4X (6 lb. test) to 6X (3 lb. test) tippet for most freshwater applications. If you have to pick just one size, I recommend 5X (4 lb. test) for freshwater fishing. In salt water or for larger fish like salmon or steelhead, use something a bit heavier, from 1X (12 lb. test) to 03X (22 lb. test). Here again, the tippet size should be heavy enough to toss a large fly to a fish without twisting into knots—and heavy enough to withstand the forces of a strong fish—yet light enough to fool the fish into thinking the fly is free-floating, not one tied to a fishing line.

Use the accompanying table as a guide for matching hook (fly) and tippet sizes. For example, sizes 14 and 16 flies are ideal for 5X tippet, although sizes 18 and 12 flies might also be used in a pinch.

TIPPET	8X	7X	6X	5X	4X	3X	2X	1X	0X	01X	02X	03X
POUND TEST	1	2	3	4	6	8	10	12	14	16	19	22
FLY SIZES	28–24	24–20	20–16	18–12	14–10	12–8	10–6	8–4	6–2	4–1/0	1/0–2/0	3/0–5/0

Chest Waders and Wading Staffs

Some of my friends like to wet-wade, or wade in their sandals, sneakers, or bare feet. However, since I may fish for five or more hours in a day, I prefer more protection for my tender feet and to keep them dry. Waders made of breathable fabrics are fine for most fishing, but in early spring or winter or when the water is really cold, I like my 5 mm neoprene waders. When I fish close to home I use boot-foot waders, which are quick to pull on and off. Boots with felt soles tend to grip the bottom more securely. If these felts are also studded, so much the better. When I travel, I use stocking-foot waders with lightweight wading shoes. Again, felt soles—with or without studs—will help you grip the stream bottom. Korkers makes heavy-duty studded wading sandals that you can strap on over your boots when the stream bottom is especially slippery.

For additional insulation, wear fleece pants that have stirrups. The stirrups prevent the pant legs from riding up and binding your legs, which will reduce circulation. Good, comfortable wading socks will also make a long day in your waders a lot more pleasant, especially in places where considerable walking is necessary. Last, Hodgman has recently introduced a breathable wader with a waterproof front zipper that we coffee drinkers find especially useful!

Whenever you go fishing in unknown waters, bring along a collapsible wading staff. There are several good ones available, like the Folstaf with built-in compass and the folding staff made by Fulcrum. If you get into a tough situation while wading, a good staff will help you get back to safety without filling your chest waders with water. An old ski pole or even a simple sturdy stick are adequate stand-ins for a wading staff if you're on a tight budget.

Clothing and Other Accessories

So far, I have mentioned rods, reels, fly line, and waders. I also recommend you purchase or otherwise procure dry-fly floatant, nippers or small

What to Do If Your Waders Fill with Water

When you wear waders, always tighten your wader belt. If you do step into water that's over the top of your waders, the belt will slow the flow of water into your waders and give you some time to get your situation under control. Contrary to popular belief, waders that are full of water won't make you sink. While you may not be able to swim easily, you can still float on your back. Whatever you do, don't panic. Remain on your back and float downstream, feet first, using your arms to guide you. When you reach a spot where you can firmly touch bottom, simply lower your legs and walk out of the stream.

As you gain dry land, you'll notice the weight of the water that's filled your boots. A cubic foot of water weighs about sixty pounds on dry land, and that's about what you'll be carrying. With a bit of luck, it will be a warm summer day and you might enjoy the experience. If the weather is cool or cold, however, get to a warm, dry area as soon as possible. Empty your waders and, if dry clothes are not available, put the waders back on; they will provide a layer of insulation. Don't fool around: in cold weather you're at risk for hypothermia, which is potentially lethal. Get help as soon as you can and get out of there.

fingernail clippers—which you'll use to trim excess tippet when tying on flies—and small hemostats or forceps to help you remove a stubborn fly from the mouth of a toothy fish. Having some of these tools on zingers, or retractable cords, will keep them conveniently out of the way. Wear bronze-tinted polarized sunglasses and a wide-brim hat to protect you from the sun or perhaps an errantly cast fly. If you designate a hat specifically for fishing you may, like me, be less likely to forget it as you head out to your favorite fishing spots. My hat has an adjustable chinstrap that keeps it on my head, plus it has a built in foam pad that will keep it afloat should it be blown off. A white or off-white hat may give fish the impression of clouds and probably won't spook them, whereas you should avoid wearing bright-colored hats.

A lightweight backpack will hold your lunch, a small coffee thermos, extra water, and snacks. Into this pack you can stash an extra travel rod and reel, extra tippet and leaders, a small flashlight, stick insect repellent, sunblock or tanning lotion, compass, whistle, a small first-aid kit, spare socks, ziplock bags, waterproof matches, and a camera with extra batteries. Remember, in a pinch a large plastic trash bag can be made into an effective rain jacket.

Clothing

Speaking of rain jackets, now would be a good time to address the matter of clothing. When choosing from the myriad specialty fishing shirts and pants that are on the market, the first rule of thumb is go for comfort. Long-sleeve shirts provide better sun and insect protection. Some new fabrics contain built-in sun protection, and a fabric by Ex Officio also offers insect protection that will endure more than thirty washings. It also helps if the fabric dries quickly and has adequate ventilation.

While some shirts look great at the lodge or around camp, it's best to avoid wearing bright colors when fishing, particularly red and yellow. Remember, fish have excellent color vision. Although the refractive index of water makes objects appear flatter as the distance between those objects and the fish increases, to a fish, you may appear to be nothing more than a red wafer. But, since it probably doesn't see a red wafer every day, the fish may prefer to stay away from you than eat. This is not good. What's worse is, each time you move that red-sleeved arm of yours to cast, you risk spooking the fish. A fish can really get nervous when it sees an odd-colored wafer with a casting arm! I once saw this happen while I was fishing for bonefish with my son. He wore a bright-yellow fishing shirt, and when he made a cast I could see the distant bonefish react to his movement.

If you must wear bright-colored clothing, you can reduce its spook potential by moving slowly and fishing upstream. But even this may not always be possible. Instead, wear subdued colors that are natural to the fishing area. Browns, tans, and greens are usually safe colors. Whites and grays may work on cloudy days, and aqua might work on tropical flats. In areas where the fish get a lot of pressure, using fly line in neutral, less bright colors will reduce spook potential even more.

When traveling, I like to take along fleece and synthetic clothing, including synthetic tee shirts and underpants. In addition to wicking away body moisture, these fabrics dry much faster than cotton, often overnight if you wash them the night before. On long trips, take along a backup pair of fleece pants and an extra fleece jacket, and always tuck in a quality, breathable, dark-colored rain jacket even if the forecast is for clear weather.

Flies

You'll note that there is one rather glaring item missing from this fly tackle discussion so far—flies. Hopefully, you'll progress through this book and begin tying your own flies, starting with the four described in Hours 21–24, An Introduction to Fly Tying. However, anticipating that your need is more critical, I'll recommend some flies you might consider purchasing.

But first let me demystify the system used to indicate hook sizes. The freshwater hook system uses even numbers from 2 to 28 to indicate size, whereby the larger the number, the smaller the hook. For example, a size 28 hook is really, really tiny. A size 2 hook is fairly large, and it has a hook gap—the distance between the hook shank and the point—that's about the size of a dime. Beyond a size 2 hook, convention changes a bit and saltwater hook numbering takes over. Common saltwater hook sizes start at 1/0, 2/0, 3/0 and continue to increase in size using the X/0 designation. If you're going for bluegill, trout, and similar-size panfish, hook sizes 20 to 12 ought to suit you nicely. If you're trying to catch largemouth and smallmouth bass, larger hook sizes to size 2 may be more appropriate. Saltwater fish are generally larger, so for the most part your hook size will

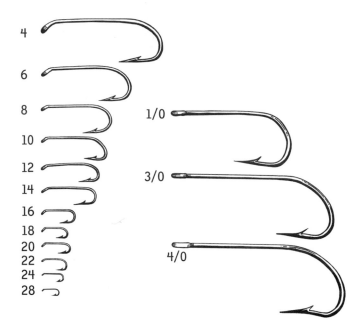

Hook size comparisons.

also increase. For example, good hook sizes for striped bass, bluefish, and redfish might be 1/0 or 2/0. For bonefish, which have a smaller mouth, the smaller size 6 or 8 hooks may be more effective.

The accompanying table lists some basic freshwater and saltwater flies. While there are other patterns you may wish to have in your fly box, these will at least get you started and give you a decent shot at catching fish.

Nothing in this table is absolute; it's only a guide. Your best bet is to ask someone at your local tackle shop which flies they recommend for the type of fishing you'll be doing. You could also contact someone from a local fly-fishing club to get the latest information on the hot fly. If you're fishing in an unknown area, such as when you travel, find the local fly shop. You'll probably have to get a fishing license anyway, and it would be a good opportunity to get information and any special flies or other items that are known to work well in that area. Often these shops serve as a daily gathering place for many anglers, and the owner probably can orient you to the area quickly.

FRESHWATER PATTERN	HOOK SIZE	PATTERN COLOR	SALTWATER PATTERN	HOOK SIZE	PATTERN COLOR
Woolly Bugger	4–6	black, olive, teal	Clouser	2, 1/0, 2/0	white/chartreuse, black, black/white
Black Gnat Parachute or Parachute Adams	12–14	black gray	Deceiver	2, 1/0, 2/0	black, blue/white, green/white
Bead-Head Hares Mask Nymphs	12–14	brown	Surf Candy	1/0	black, chartreuse, green/white
Elk-Hair Caddis	12, 14, 16	tan, dark brown	Crazy Charlie	4, 6, 8	brown, pink, tan
CDC Emergers	16, 18	tan, gray	Shrimp	2, 4, 1/0	olive, gold

TIP: If a shop owner provides helpful information about where to fish and which flies or other equipment to use, please be sure to reward him by purchasing something from his shop. The gesture will please him, and he might just give you that gem of information you need to have a great trip.

Creating a Shopping List

If you're new to fly-fishing, you'll have to develop a shopping list of the equipment you need. The equipment list in the Appendix of this book will give you a place to start. Carefully go over this list and determine the rod, reel, and line sizes that will give you a balanced outfit. If you're on a tight budget, you may have to prioritize a bit. Your priorities should be a high-quality fly line, a good rod, a decent reel, backing, leaders, some extra tippet, a fly box, flies, and polarized sunglasses. You can add other items as needed or as your budget allows.

(continued next page)

Make an inventory of what you might already have that will work, like clothing. Take it from this avid angler who, after falling in the water, has fished naked in his chest waders: clothing is not the highest priority. Joking aside, you may very well have clothing in your closet that will suffice for now.

If you decide to buy tapered leaders, buy a couple in each size. For freshwater fishing, 4X, 5X, and 6X will cover most situations. For saltwater fishing, 2X–02X will give you latitude to catch many coastal species. If you'll be chasing bluefish or similar species, be sure to buy some extra-strong, protected tapered leaders that are specially made for fish with sharp teeth.

You can get just about all you need in one stop at places like Gander Mountain, Cabelas, or a Bass Pro Shop. You can consider purchasing your equipment online, but you won't get the same service you can expect from a small retail shop. Plus, you can't *feel* the equipment or compare products. If you live near one of the big stores I mentioned above, you're in luck. If not, your best alternative is to find a local fly tackle shop where you may very well get the best service and, overall, the best deal. The folks at local shops can be especially helpful if you're pressed for time and need help making critical equipment decisions.

Time Check

If all has gone according to plan, you have acquired the basic fly-fishing equipment you need. I hope your shopping excursion was enjoyable and you were able to pick up a few bargains along the way. Perhaps you're even ahead of schedule and are standing there admiring your purchases. You may be wondering what you're going to do with all this stuff. Next, I will teach you the knots you will use to put it all together.

HURS 6–7

TYING KNOTS AND ASSEMBLING
THE FLY-FISHING TACKLE

Knots can make or break you! I once knew a fellow who advocated that if you can't tie good knots, tie a lot of them. I cannot endorse this philosophy; I have seen too many great fish lost because of a poorly tied knot. I routinely use the knots I describe in this chapter whenever I go fishing. I have tested the heck out of them, and each has an important purpose. That said, if you prefer to use a different knot in any case described below because that's how you were taught, or you already know and like a particular knot, go ahead and use it. If you ever want to try something new, however, these knots will be waiting for you.

I describe only six knots in this chapter, and I've arranged them in the order in which you'll tie them when you assemble your tackle. You can tie three of the knots at home, using the instructions as needed for reference. You'll use the other three in the field, so you must commit them to memory. Practice these knots until you can tie them habitually. If you absolutely must have an instruction reference in the field, make yourself a cheat sheet, laminate it, and carry it in your pocket. When you're tying on a fly, no one will even notice that you're using a reference card.

Before we get started, here are a couple of knot-tying terms. The end of the line that you'll work with is called the *tag end*. When you finish tying your knot and pull it tight, you generally trim this end. The main length of line is called the *standing part*.

TIP: Almost every knot will reduce the breaking strength of your line by about 15 percent. When fighting or attempting to land a fish, take this reduced break strength into account before you brutishly force the fish in.

ARBOR KNOT

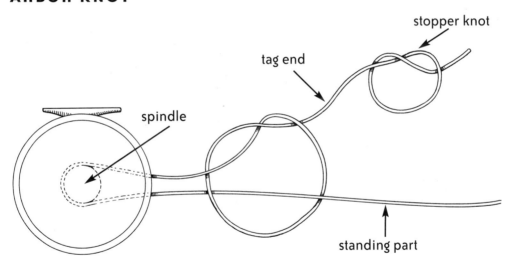

Arbor knot.

The arbor knot is the simplest knot fishers use to attach the fly line backing to the spindle on the reel. It consists of two overhand knots. The second knot, called the stopper knot, prevents the first knot from coming undone, which in turn prevents the tag end of the backing from slipping off the reel. For this discussion, the reel is mounted on the assembled rod and is positioned so it hangs from the cork handle.

1. Feed the backing through all the rod guides and run it into the reel at the bottom. Thread the tag end around the spindle, over the top, and back out of the reel.
2. With the tag end tie an overhand knot around the standing part of the line.
3. About an inch or less above the first knot, tie the stopper knot.
4. Pull the standing part of the line to draw the knot tight. The knot should be firm around the reel's spindle, or arbor.
5. Trim the tag end of the line.

NAIL KNOT

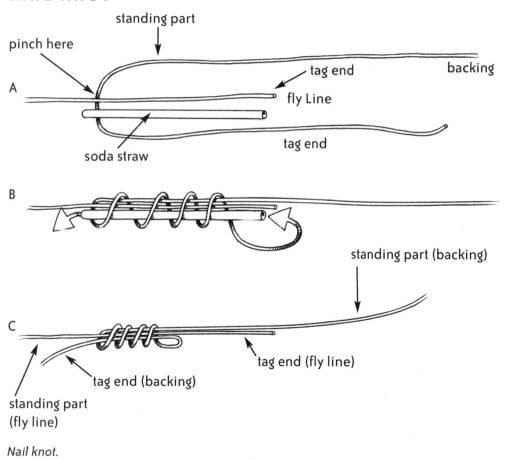

Nail knot.

This is the most complex knot I will ask you to learn. Use it to connect the fly line to the backing. Before you start, get a 2-inch length of a soda straw or similar hollow tube. Also, while not absolutely necessary, a small amount of Pliobond cement is useful for sealing the knot when you're finished tying it. You may also want to solicit a friend's help with Step 1. The extra hands can be useful.

1. Pinch the fly line, straw, and backing near where they cross the standing part of the fly line (A). Perhaps your friend can hold the tag end, the other end of the straw, and the running part of the backing.
2. With the tag end, make four complete turns around the fly line and straw, and then insert the end into the straw (B). Push the end toward the area you're pinching and through the end of the straw. You may have to ease your pinch to allow the end of the line to pass through the end of the straw.
3. When you have the tag end in hand, remove the straw.
4. Slowly draw the nail knot tight. Take your time. It helps to roll the knot between your fingers, which allows the four turns of the backing to align and seat themselves. It also helps to moisten the knot before you really draw it up tight, and to alternately pull the tag end of the fly line against the tag end of the backing.
5. Pull the standing part of the backing against the standing part of the fly line. With each alternating pull, you can add more tension until the knot is well seized (C).
6. Make one last pull with the standing parts of both lines. If they hold, trim the tag ends close to the knot and apply Pliobond cement.

DOUBLE SURGEON'S LOOP

This is the quickest and easiest loop you'll tie. Its biggest weakness is that it's a relatively weak knot. *Do not use this loop for your tippet;* instead, use it only at the butt end (thickest part) of your tapered leader. However, after the tapered leader has been shortened by multiple fly substitutions (it may be 7' now), I also use this loop at the terminal end of the leader

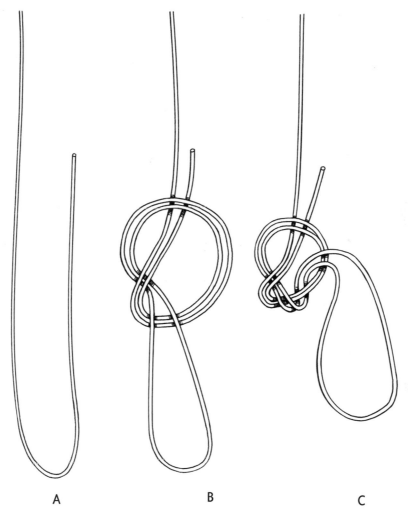

A   B   C

Double surgeon's loop.

before I add a length of tippet (functionally returning the leader to its original 9' length).

1. Make a loop (A).
2. Use the loop to tie one overhand knot (B).
3. Follow through with one more turn (C).

FOUR-TWIST LOOP

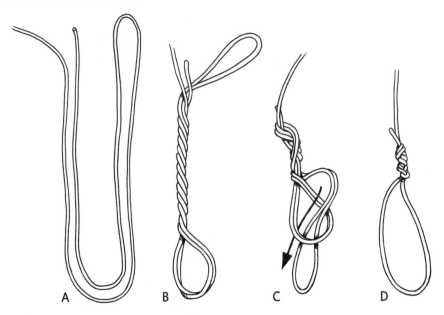

Four-twist loop.

Each time you tie on another fly, you will use up several inches of your leader. Now, let's say your 9-foot 5X tapered leader has been reduced to 7 feet through the course of a morning of fishing. We will need to add about 2 feet of 5X tippet to lengthen it to its original 9 feet. To do this, tie a double surgeon's loop to the leader's end. Note this end should have a slightly larger diameter than the tippet we are about to add. Cut about 30 inches of tippet from a spool of 5X tippet and tie a much stronger four-twist loop knot at one end.

Although this tippet loop knot is a bit more difficult to tie, it's stronger and less likely to break when you have a big fish on than the double surgeon's loop.

1. With about 30 inches of tippet in your hand, make a double loop that's about 4 inches long (A).
2. Pinch the double loop in the center, then stick your finger in the lower loop and twist it four times (B).

3. Remove your finger, and then carefully pull down the single top loop so it passes through the bottom double loop (C).

4. Moisten the double loop and bring it up slowly and tightly by simultaneously pulling the single loop down and pulling the standing and tag ends of the tippet.

5. After the knot is tight, cut the tag end (D).

LOOP-TO-LOOP CONNECTION

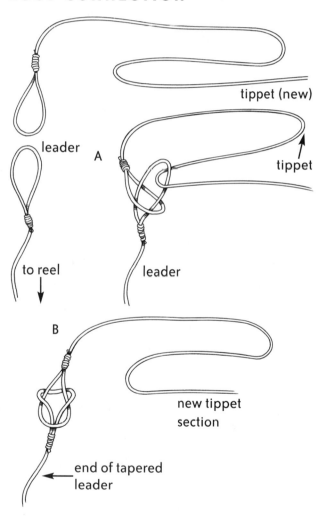

Loop-to-loop connection.

When the knot is finished you will be ready to make a loop-to-loop connection with the terminal loop of the leader.

1. Insert the leader's double surgeon's loop into the four-twist loop of the tippet (A).
2. Insert the terminal end of the tippet into the double surgeon's loop and pull it all the way through (B).
3. Pull both knots together to form what resembles a square knot.

LANYARD LOOP

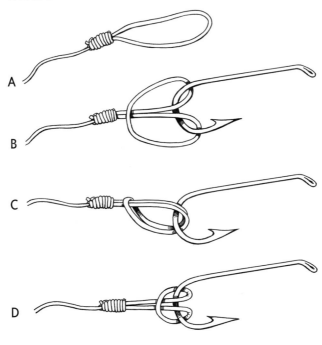

Lanyard loop.

Use this simple knot to attach a second, or tandem, fly to another fly.

1. Use the four-twist loop to make a loop in 25 to 30 inches of tippet (A).
2. Form a double loop by simply folding over the single loop.
3. Pass the hook through each of the double loops (B), and draw the knot tight (C, D).

This knot only works well with barbed hooks. It is also easy to untie should your line tangle. (By taking the second hook off the line, it's sometimes easier to get everything straightened out.) For tandem rigging barbless hooks, use Sousa's four-turn knot, described next.

SOUSA'S FOUR-TURN KNOT

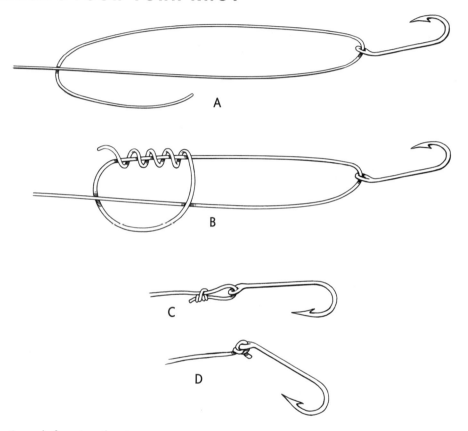

Sousa's four-turn knot.

Use this knot to tie on your fly. It's smaller, stronger, and faster to tie than the popular "improved" clinch knot. Indeed, the reason I like this knot better is because it's the fastest knot I can tie—an especially important consideration when your hands are cold. It's a very secure knot, and its high amount of strength retains much of the original tippet or tapered leader strength.

1. Insert the terminal, or tag end, of your tippet into the eye of the hook.
2. With the hook on the line and in your right hand, form a loop by leading the tag end back alongside the standing part (A).
3. With your left hand, bring the tag end toward you, beneath the standing part, and upward. Note that you have now formed a secondary loop and that the primary loop is holding the fly.
4. With the tip of the tag end, make four overhand turns on the secondary loop, working back toward the reel (B).
5. Hold the tip of the tag end and the standing part firmly, moisten, and draw the knot tight (C). It should form a sliding knot that's drawn tightly to the hook (D).

As you draw the knot up, you may feel a pop. This is a very good thing, as the pop indicates you're approaching 100 percent of its tested potential to resist breaking. After the pop, some of the knot actually enters the hook's eye, which better distributes the stress and lessens the pinch on the standing part of the line. Years ago, I had an opportunity to test this knot on a line tension machine and was very pleased with the results.

For size 4 hooks and larger, you may wish to add an overhand stopper knot on the tag end. Sousa's four-turn knot can sometimes slip out of hooks made from heavier gauge wire, especially if you use ultra-slippery fluorocarbon leaders and tippet to tie the knot. You can reduce most slipping by making sure the knot is moistened and seizes together well during tightening. The stopper knot is just cheap insurance when a really big fish is on your hook.

Putting It All Together

Now that you have your gear and you've learned the knots, let's assemble everything so you can get out there and fish. I'll assume that you have a 5- or 6-weight fly rod, a reel, a spool of backing and some WF6F fly line, a tapered leader, and some tippet. Also, you have some flies. Now, get some Pliobond cement from your hardware store and, if a preformed terminal loop didn't come with your fly line, ask your tackle dealer to give you a few yards of 30 or 40 lb. test monofilament fishing line. With these items assembled, we are ready to tie everything together.

Prepare the rod and reel.

There are two ways to add line onto a reel: the wrong way and the correct way. To get it right, put the rod together and align the guides up and down the rod. Before mounting the fly reel onto the rod, set the drag to its nearly full position. You can determine the direction of the drag when you turn the handle in one direction. There should be more resistance than when you turn the handle the other way. Mount the reel facing down on the fly rod such that when you pull the line out of the bottom of the reel, you can feel the reel's drag resisting (see the arbor knot illustration, page 44). Note that if you feel drag resistance as you reel line back in, you need to stop and take all the line off the reel and wind it in the other direction.

Determine how much backing you need.

One way to figure out how much backing you need is to reverse the process: temporarily wind the fly line on the reel first and then add backing to the remaining space to fill the spool. When you can't wind any more backing onto the spool you know you have enough. Now remove a small amount of backing until the reel can turn freely. At this point, with the reel full you can cut the backing.

Next, reverse the backing and fly line. As dubious as it may seem, you start by taking all the line off the reel. This process can be easier if you have a rotating drum on which to store the line. If not, *carefully* lay all the line on your floor. I emphasize *carefully* because the length of the line can create all kinds of tangles. If you can, spread the line out on a large area of bare floor, and be sure to keep the dog, cat, and small children out of the room until you're finished reversing the line and the reel is filled once again.

When you're ready, thread the end of the backing through all the rod guides, starting with the tiptop guide. Push the end into the reel near the bottom and through the reel's line guides if they're present. Use the arbor knot to tie the backing onto the spindle.

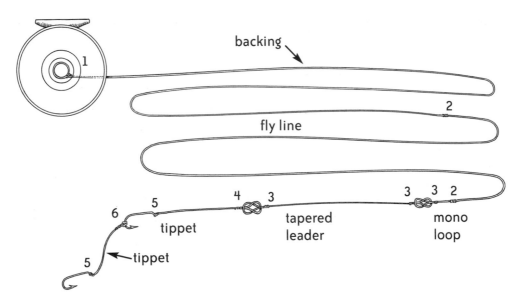

1) Arbor Knot; 2) Nail Knot; 3) Double Surgeon's Loop; 4) Four-Twist Loop; 5) Sousa's Four-Turn Knot; 6) Lanyard Loop Knot. (Illustration not drawn to scale.)

Mount the backing on the spool.

Use the arbor knot (see page 44) to secure the backing to the fly reel's spindle, and start cranking the backing onto the spool. To reiterate, the backing should be coming off the bottom of the reel. If you're cranking the reel against the drag, you have mounted the backing in the wrong direction.

TIP: To mount the backing evenly across the width of the spool, wind it in a zig-zag fashion such that it doesn't pile up in one spot on the spool.

Connect the fly line and reel it onto the spool.

Use the nail knot to connect the reel end of the fly line to the backing. Give the knot a little tug to test its integrity. You may decide to seal it with

Pliobond cement. Other cement may do the job, but Pliobond's flexibility resists cracking.

TIP: Many fly line manufacturers use a sticky tab to identify the reel end of the fly line. If yours isn't identified, attach the thin end to the backing. The other end—the end that you'll be casting—has a much thicker taper in the first thirty feet of line.

Fly line usually comes in a neat coil. To pay out your fly line, unfurl it one turn at a time. If you merely lay the whole coil on the floor and wind it onto your reel, a tangled mess is sure to result. Go slowly, and hold the entire coil in your hand as you unwind it one coil at a time.

Line twist or kinking may occur as you add fly line to the reel. You can reduce kinking by sliding the whole coil of fly line onto a soup can and then allow the coil to rotate around the can as you reel the line onto the spool. Ask a friend to hold the can horizontally while you crank the fly line onto the spool. Remember: to avoid tangles, work slowly.

Stop reeling the fly line about a yard or two before the terminal loop— to which you'll attach your leader—reaches the rod tip. Some manufacturers provide premounted loops on their fly lines, while others may give you a loop to mount yourself. I highly recommend one of these fly lines. Simply follow the manufacturer's instructions for mounting their fly line loops.

Loops are not included with all fly lines, however, so you may have to make your own. This is easy if you have a 2- to 3-foot piece of 30 or 40 lb. test monofilament fishing line.

1. Use a nail knot to connect the monofilament line to the terminal end of the fly line. By the time you're finished, you will have added at least a foot or two of length to your fly line.
2. Within 2 inches of the fly line, tie a small double surgeon's loop in the monofilament line.
3. Trim the excess monofilament line, and seal the nail knot with Pliobond cement.

Attach the leader.

Leaders can be expensive, so be careful how you uncoil one from the package. You don't want to start off with any strength-reducing knots. At the thicker, butt end, tie a small double surgeon's loop that's no more than 1 inch long. Then trim the tag end.

Make a loop-to-loop connection to attach the leader to the fly line loop (see illustration, page 49). Insert the loop on the fly line—which is on the reel side of things—into the loop on the leader. I remember this convention by saying to myself, "Reel in" as the reel-side loop goes into the other loop.

Tie on the fly.

Although the illustration indicates that you attach the tippet next, you only have to attach a tippet if you've been fishing for a while and need to extend your leader. I'll describe how that all works shortly. For now, let's say you've just arrived at your favorite fishing hole and you have ample leader on which to tie your fly. Use Sousa's four-turn knot to tie the fly onto the leader.

Attach the tippet.

Let's say you've been out fishing for a few hours and have changed flies several times. Not only has your leader length been reduced—let's say from 9 feet to about 7 feet—but the taper at the end of your original leader has also been reduced, we'll say from 5X to the equivalent of 4X. Rather than tie on another costly leader, now is the time to tie on a few feet of relatively inexpensive tippet, and here's what you do.

1. Tie a small double surgeon's loop into the 4X end of the leader.
2. Cut thirty inches of 5X tippet from the spool. At one end, tie a small (about one inch) four-twist loop, then trim any excess from the tag end.
3. Use the loop-to-loop connection to connect the two loops.

Simple. Now you have a 2-foot 5X extension on your leader and you're ready to roll again. When it's time to add more tippet later, all you have to do is cut one side of the four-turn loop on the original tippet and simply pull the old tippet section off. Then repeat the sequence above to add a new tippet section.

A Few More Tips

Before we wrap up this business of knots and tackle assembly and move on to casting, let me offer some other tips. It should take only a few minutes to review these. And if everything you've learned and practiced so far has gone smoothly, we should still have plenty of time to get through everything else in this book, right on schedule!

▸ **Reduce friction.** The act of tightening a knot generates a small amount of heat, which can reduce the strength of your line. Wet each knot with a bit of water as you're pulling it tight. The moisture will help dissipate that heat, and it will also act as a lubricant as you draw the knot tight.

▸ **Prepare.** If you find time on your hands at the camp, tie several tippet lengths and store them for future use.

▸ **Take precautions.** When I tie on large saltwater flies, I sometimes tie a simple overhand knot at the tag end to serve as a stopper knot. The stopper knot can prevent your terminal knot from slipping off the hook when you get a big fish on.

▸ **Choose the right material.** Fluorocarbon is very slippery, transparent underwater, and is somewhat different from regular monofilament fishing line. If you use fluorocarbon for your leaders or tippets, add an extra twist or turn to your knots to help them hold. Taking this extra step may save that big fish.

▸ **Loop it.** Double surgeon's loops are easier to tie than four-twist loops, *and* they aren't as strong. To compensate, tie double surgeon's loops at the butt (thicker) end of the line, which is stronger than your smaller diameter tippet. Use the four-twist loop to add tippet, which has a lower breaking strength than the shortened and terminal part of your leader. With practice, the four-twist loop will become quite simple to tie.

▸ **Avoid knots.** So-called wind knots result from poor casting technique and they weaken the breaking strength of leaders and tippets considerably. Avoid them as best you can. If you find that your lines are producing a lot of wind knots, however, don't fret; even the best anglers get them on occasion. If you can untie them, great. If not, you might have to bite the bullet and tie on another piece of tippet. Don't trust a tippet with a wind knot.

▸ **Cut or Untangle?** When faced with any tangled line, assess about how long it will take to untangle it. If you think you can tie another piece of line on faster or more easily, that may be the best way to go. Designate a pocket for your excess pieces of leader, tippet, and other debris, and properly dispose of this trash later.

H🕐URS 8–9

CASTING WITH A FLY ROD

In the course of teaching thousands of Boy Scouts how to successfully cast, I learned some critical lessons. First among these is that casting can be broken down into four essential components, each so easy that, by following this sequence, you'll be roll casting and casting in the traditional way with gleeful accuracy within a few minutes. I'll go over each component in turn, and I ask only that you take no short cuts, no matter how tempted you might be.

To start, let me offer a couple of suggestions. First, using a Sharpie or line marker, make a permanent, $\frac{1}{2}$-inch-long mark on the fly line thirty feet back from the loop end. Also, take a moment to stretch out any kinks or memory curls in this front section of the fly line. This can be done by firmly pulling short lengths of fly line between your hands to straighten it out. Do this for the first thirty feet of line.

In a large class, students line up and practice casting together. Often they can learn a lot just by watching their fellow classmates.

The Four Essential Components of Casting

My goal in this section is to teach you to cast thirty feet of fly line in a straight line toward a target using a roll cast and a traditional cast. With components 1 and 2, you will be able to make a roll cast. By adding components 3 and 4, you will be able to make the beautiful tight-looped traditional casts you've seen in the movies.

Note: I strongly suggest you master the roll cast before you begin working on the traditional cast; however, for the purpose of introducing the four components in sequence, we'll look at the traditional cast first. I also suggest that you practice casting in your backyard if access to water is not convenient. Don't use a fly when casting on land; instead, use a 5-foot length of 10 lb. test monofilament fishing line with a ½-inch piece of colorful yarn tied at its end. This will simulate a tapered leader and fly.

Component 1: Thumb and Finger Movement

Place the thumb of your casting hand on top of the cork handle, or grip. You do this because the thumb—the strongest digit—provides the forward driving power in both the traditional cast and the roll cast (which we'll discuss later). So, when casting, make this your mantra: lift (the rod) with the fingers, power forward with the thumb. Think "up with your fingers and forward with your thumb."

Component 1. Notice the placement of the thumb at the top of the fly rod handle. Also note how the fingers are pinching the fly line. Pinching the line like this prevents additional line from unspooling during practice casts.

Component 2: The 1 O'Clock and 10 O'Clock Stopping Points

During the back cast, the stopping point of the rod tip is always at 1 o'clock. (The noon position is your head; the 1 o'clock position is just a few degrees behind it.) On the forecast, the stopping point is 10 o'clock. (The 10 o'clock "stopping point" is really more of a pause to allow the forward loop to form.)

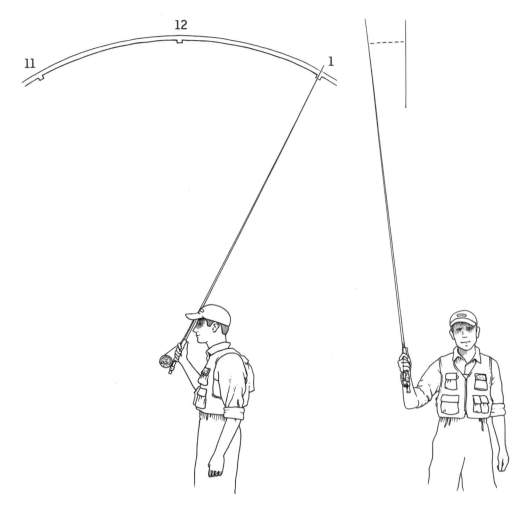

Component 2. *The rod tip is in the 1 o'clock position (left). Notice how the rod tip is angled outward from the angler (right).*

Component 3: Loading the Rod

Bending or loading the rod with the weight of your line and tackle is a crucial component to achieve casting distance. (See the sidebar on page 64 for a more detailed look at why.) To load the rod, point the rod tip close to, but not quite touching, the surface of the water. At this point, you'll want to pinch the fly line to the grip with the middle finger of your casting hand (see photo page 61). This will prevent line from unspooling while you cast.

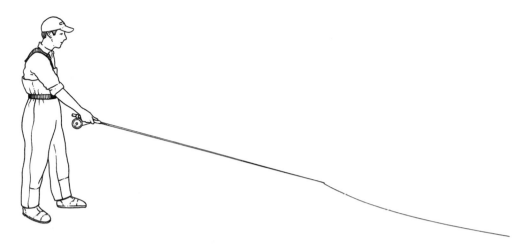

Component 3. *When preparing to make a backcast, point the rod tip downward toward the water. Stand in a comfortable position that will allow you to shift your balance from your front foot to your rear foot. You will shift your weight to the front foot again as you make your forecast.*

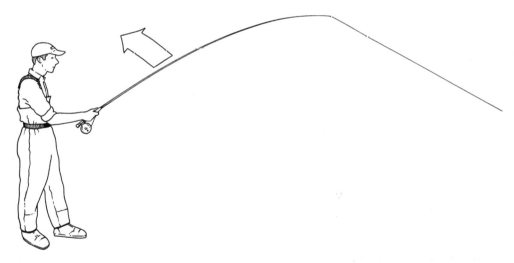

Component 3 (continued). *You don't have to rip the line off the water as you begin to lift it. Start slow and increase the speed as you progress through the cast.*

Next, lift the rod tip to draw the fly line slowly off the water, then, with increasing speed, lift the rod tip and snap stop at the 1 o'clock position. (Note: If the fly makes a bubble and pops when you lift it off the water, you know that you are going too fast.) You know you're getting enough power into the lift when, after the snap-stop, the fly line completely unfurls behind you and hangs in the air for a moment before dropping to the ground. (At this point, for the purposes of practicing, it's OK to let the line fall to the ground behind you.)

TIP: If you don't seem to have the initial strength to lift the rod tip with your casting hand, try placing your other hand just below the reel seat. The added strength of the second hand is often all you need to get the line up and flying.

Sometimes two hands are better than one.

Casting: A Transfer of Energy

Here's a tidbit for those of you with an engineering bent. The fly rod is a transducer. During the initial lift of the line from the water, *kinetic*, or *movement*, energy starts to transfer from the rod to the line. When the rod tip reaches the abrupt stop at the 1 o'clock position, energy transfers to the line, allowing the line to unfurl behind you. When you begin to bring the rod tip forward, the energy starts to transfer from the line back to the rod through a process called *loading*. The stored potential energy in the rod then begins to transfer back into the line. When the rod tip reaches the 10 o'clock position and stops, all of the energy is released to the line again, and the terminal end to which the fly is attached gracefully unfurls forward over the water. Fly rod and fly line manufacturers spend a lot of research-and-development dollars on making lines and rods that work together.

Component 4: The Forecast

The last component is an important one. Get this right, and you'll produce a tight loop and deliver your fly accurately. Then you can marvel at your casting success.

With the line flying out behind you after your snap-stop (see illustration page 66), you have to wait until the line completely unfurls before beginning the forward cast. The best way to learn the timing of this is to watch the line unfurl. After your snap-stop, keep the rod tip in the 1 o'clock position; don't move it. Look over your shoulder and watch the fly line as it loops and rolls away from you. At the instant when it's fully unfurled, flat and parallel to the ground, and about to fall, apply firm pressure with your thumb and push the rod tip forward to the 10 o'clock stopping point. It really is that simple. Get the backcast right and your forecast will automatically be correct!

Putting It All Together: Making the Traditional Cast

Now that you know the four components of casting, let's briefly string them together into a sequence.

1. Point your rod tip toward the water's surface.
2. Move the rod backward to lift the line off the water.
3. Snap-stop the rod at the 1 o'clock position.
4. Allow the line to fully unfurl behind you and hover in the air for an instant.
5. Move the rod forward and pause at the 10 o'clock position.
6. Let the fly line fall to the water. (The fly will always go in the direction you point the rod tip.)

The Roll Cast

The roll cast uses only the first two components described above. Again, for that reason, you might practice the roll cast first, then work your way up to a traditional cast.

Component 4. *After the rod tip is snap-stopped, the fly line begins to form a rearward-moving loop. Before beginning your forecast, you must wait until the loop fully unfurls behind you.*

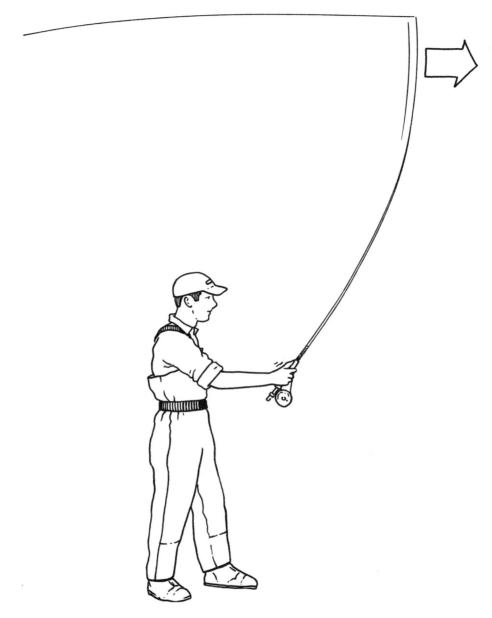

Component 4 (continued). *Note the bend in the rod during the forward part of the cast. The energy from the rearward movement of the line combines with the energy exerted by the thumb, and together they load the rod like a spring. When you pause the rod at the 10 o'clock position during the forecast, the energy transfers to the fly line, and off it goes in the direction you point your rod tip.*

The roll cast can be used to pay out additional fly line or to straighten the line on the water prior to lifting for a traditional backcast (as described above in Component 3). A roll cast is also used when brush, trees, rocks, or some obstructions to your rear prevent you from successfully executing a backcast.

A roll cast should enable you to reach fish thirty feet away or more. Here's how:

1. Start with about 25 or 30 feet of fly line on the water (or your lawn). The permanent mark you made on the fly line should be right at the rod tip. For the purposes of this exercise, you should also be pinching the fly line against the grip with the middle finger of your casting hand so that no additional line is pulled from the reel while you are casting (see the figure depicting Component 1). Check the position of your thumb to be sure it's at the top of the grip. Now *slowly* raise the rod tip to the 1 o'clock position.

2. With the reel pointing directly at the water, tilt the rod tip slightly to your side. Take a breath; there's no need to hurry. Now flick your wrist forward, pushing with your thumb, while moving the rod tip toward the 10 o'clock position. Some anglers compare the motion with that of hammering a nail. Exert the most forward power from 1 o'clock to 10 o'clock. The rod tip should pause momentarily at the 10 o'clock position before fading lower as it follows the fly line's path outward and toward the water.

Practice this exercise several times until it becomes easy. If you have difficulty casting 30 feet of fly line, try shortening your casts to 20 or 25 feet.

Once you've mastered the roll cast, you can go on to learn the graceful traditional cast that you've seen in the movies.

A Few More Things to Bear in Mind

Although I've allotted two hours for learning how to cast a fly rod, you should be able to learn the sequence in just a few minutes. Practice will take some time—and you *should* practice until your casting skills are proficient. Before we move on to the next chapter, however, here are some other casting pointers and bits of advice to keep in mind.

Again, It's OK to Look Back at Your Fly Line

Looking back at your fly line as it unfurls is not only OK, it is encouraged. Looking back will help you learn the correct time to begin your forecast. Remember, if you make a good backcast, your forecast will almost always be good.

Timing Is Everything

I was once asked by a scout leader who wanted to know if it's the wrist, forearm, upper arm, or shoulder that has the most influence on good casting. My answer? None of the above. With casting, the most effective muscle is your brain! Get the timing of your forecast down, and you'll see that it isn't *how much* power you put behind the cast but *when* you exert the power that's most important.

TIP: Thanks to the way water bends light, a fish cannot see you if you're standing 35 to 40 feet away. Casting 30 feet of fly line on a 9-foot fly rod with 9 feet of leader will place your fly 48 feet away from you. At that distance, you'll be invisible to any fish rising under your fly.

The legendary Joan Wulff once won a distance casting championship with a cast exceeding 160 feet. Now, I doubt that Joan weighs an ounce more than a hundred pounds, and she is by no means a body builder. What allows Joan to cast these extraordinary distances is an impeccable sense of timing and casting technique. Great casters make casting look effortless.

In fact it almost is. Just practice your timing and let the line and rod do the work; after all, that's why you paid the big bucks to buy good equipment.

Troubleshooting

If your line cracks like a whip when you begin your forecast, you're coming forward too soon. Remember, let the line completely unfurl behind you before beginning your forecast. Remember, it is OK to look behind you as you cast.

TIP: Videotape your casting practice. You'll quickly identify any problems with your technique once you watch yourself.

This instruction bears repeating: Crisply stop your rod tip at the 1 o'clock position, then watch the line unfurl behind you. When it's fully extended start to bring it forward. Then pause the rod tip at 10 o'clock to wait for the forward loop to form. If you can do those few things, your casts will be fine.

This angler is making a side-arm cast. Note that the rod is stopped in the 1:00 position, and the fly line is forming a tight loop.

Practicing Indoors

For those of you who want to practice fly-casting technique indoors, Royal Wulff makes a wonderful teaching aid, called a Fly-O, for casting practice. The Fly-O is a 3-foot rod with 15 feet of bulky fluorescent yarn. It simulates fly tackle perfectly, and utilizes the same timing and nearly the same strength to push the yarn through the casting motions. I have used my Fly-O in my living room to teach casting technique and to improve accuracy. If you can cast with a Fly-O, your transition to a fly rod will be easy.

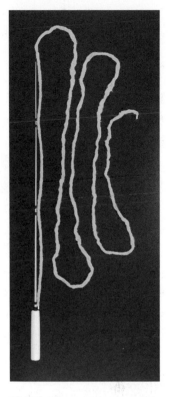

The Fly-O comes in handy for indoor practice. (Courtesy Royal Wulff)

HOUR 10

FINDING FISH

Just as in finding a good real estate investment, the key to finding fish is location, location, location. You can be sure that fish are not randomly distributed in our waterways; a fish chooses its location because its needs are being met. So, you may ask, what are some of the needs? What preferences or influences affect where fish chose to go?

The Wants and Needs of Fish

Protection

A fish's foremost need is protection. Fish want to avoid being eaten by something. They may not have a high IQ, but they probably figure out pretty early in life that many creatures great and small would enjoy eating them. That's just part of being a fish. So, above all else, most fish will go to a place where they feel less vulnerable.

Within the many thousands of fish species, there is great diversity in how they avoid being eaten. Some methods are behavioral, while others are perhaps more physiological. For example, some species form great schools whose movements and flash confuse and distract predators. Other fish develop a keen awareness of impending danger and flee quickly. Species such as flying fish actually take to the air, traveling a hundred feet or more before coming back to the water. Other species, like stickle-backs, develop long, sharp spines that extend when a predator attacks.

There are species of fish that have deceiving features, such as large eye-like spots, which can convince any passing predator that the would-be meal is actually a threat. And, of course, there are many fish that simply hide or become active only when predators aren't around.

Food

If fish spent all their time fleeing or hiding, catching them would be a lot more difficult. Fortunately for us anglers, fish do look for food, and some fish really seem to eat a lot. There are fish that spend just about all their waking hours in search of something to eat.

It's common to catch a fish whose belly is already fully extended. What could that fish possibly be thinking? Let me dispel one myth right now: fish don't think at all. They react. Fish do not have the higher-order brains that humans have and cannot possibly process the same kinds of information, such as when their bellies are uncomfortably full. When food is available fish are hardwired to take it before another fish does. Fish are greedy, plain and simple.

Reproduction

Animals need to mate and reproduce to survive, and fish have evolved numerous ways to pass their DNA on to future generations. Some fish carry many thousands of eggs, and once fertilized the eggs are set adrift as plank-ton to go wherever the tides and currents take them. Other species lay fewer eggs but protect them in nests. Some anadromous species—fish such as salmon that are hatched in fresh water and migrate to the ocean—return to fresh water during their spawning period, often carrying large, robust eggs that allow their progeny a bigger and faster, more competitive start. There is also a species of coastal shiner that has both male and female sex

The light-colored portion of the lake bottom is a bluegill nest, or redd. The term redd used to be solely associated with Atlantic salmon nests, but it is now commonly applied to nests of other fish species.

traits and can fertilize its own eggs. Once again, diversity rules, and the reproductive strategies of fish can defy the imagination.

Many sport fish are vulnerable before, during, and after reproduction—a useful condition from an angler's perspective. For example, fish may congregate in certain areas before spawning. If you learn where these areas are and when the fish will be there, you will likely find fish. However, know that as fish begin their reproductive activity, they often are so focused on mating that they won't take any presentation. But if they sense that your fly might be a competitor—albeit a small one—they might just strike it. Under these conditions you may want to use a streamer that looks a lot like a juvenile of the reproducing fish.

Strategies for Catching Fish During Spawning Season

Here's one strategy I use in Alaska to catch wild rainbow trout. Look for salmon digging nests, or redds. A salmon will turn on its side and, with its tail, make a strong slapping motion that creates a depression in the smaller rocks and cobble on the river bottom. An observant angler will see lots of insect nymphs beneath the rocks, many of which are—because of the salmon's thrashing—washing downstream to a waiting wild rainbow trout. Cast a nymph over the salmon and let it drift downstream to the trout.

If you spot a salmon that's actually spawning, use egg patterns that are the same color and size as the salmon eggs. After spawning, when the salmon is covering the redd with more rocks and gravel from an upstream position, both egg and nymph patterns can be popular with the waiting rainbow trout downstream.

Some fish, like bluegill and smallmouth bass, will vigorously protect their nests from all potential invaders. Their nests are usually circular, and the color of them contrasts with the river bottom. If you spot a nest, simply cast to it. Keep in mind, however, that these fish are vulnerable; if you catch any, be sure to get them back into the water quickly so they can resume their nursery duties and raise a new generation of fish for you to catch.

Water Temperature

Water temperature and its relationship to water's ability to retain dissolved gases, including oxygen, is critical to fish. Oxygen levels are lower in warm water, and fish have different preferences and activity levels at different water temperatures. Various species of fish have differing demands for oxygen, and if the oxygen level becomes too low, they may die. Metabolic activity, on the other hand, tends to increase with higher temperatures.

That means, if you assume that it's in its optimal thermal range, even the fussy fish you're after will quickly digest what it has eaten and will most likely feel the need to feed again soon. This is good!

During the summer months, decreasing oxygen levels are very common in freshwater rivers, lakes, and ponds, and some species—notably trout—seek out smaller, colder tributaries or perhaps underwater springs. Fish that are in warming waters are very vulnerable and may have difficulty recovering from an extended battle. Should you catch one, reel it in quickly and try to release it into well-aerated water below a riffle.

Flow Rate

Some fish seek water flow rates that give them an advantage over their prey. Predators, especially large ones, usually love current and can often be found at the mouths of rivers or coastal estuaries that flow into the lakes, bays, or the ocean.

TIP: In fast-moving water you may have to use a full-sink or sink-tip fly line or weighted flies to get down to the fish. On a stretch like this, look for slightly slower-moving water along the edges or behind logs and boulders. The current is calmer in these small areas and fish will rest or feed here. This is where you want to cast.

Generally, at higher flow rates, larger fish can maintain a controlled orientation in the water. There are times when the turbulence is so great, however, that all but the most motivated fish will be swept away. Certain species, like salmon and shad, are driven to reach upstream spawning areas. These fish are well associated with going airborne, leaping out of the water flow and over the tops of waterfalls. Often, numerous fish can be found stacked up in the plunge pool just below these impediments to upstream movement. Where legal to do so, pools just downstream of small dams are great areas to catch fish.

Water Depth

Although some fish can only be found in deep water, other species are willing to enter much shallower water when the opportunity arises. For example, when the tide is high, larger predators often move into shallow estuaries to seek prey, especially in the early evening or at dawn. Some species, like bonefish, are the first predators on the flats when the tide is rising, and they may begin moving toward deeper water just as the tide begins to fall. Fish that come into the shoals or flats are generally there to feed. From the angler's viewpoint, this is good. First, it gives us an opportunity to get to where the fish are and, second, the fish are in eating mode. As always, move slowly and quietly to avoid startling them. Also, get out at first light when fish may still be foraging close to shore.

Smell

Fish have a keen sense of smell, and they can detect and home in on very small concentrations of odors. A salmon's return to its birthplace, for example, is greatly influenced by the characteristic smell of the stream. Odor is certainly one of the major advantages live bait or other attractant baits have over artificial lures and flies.

With this in mind, make sure your flies don't give off any noxious odors that will deter fish. Be careful when you use or handle insect repellant, motorboat fuel, or other strong-smelling chemicals, especially around your streamers and wet flies. The underwater movement of these flies is their main attractant. Don't let smell work against you.

Salinity

Salinity refers to the amount of dissolved salt in water. Just like us, fish need some salt in their bodies in order to function properly. Too much salt, however, is deadly. A saltwater fish can live in the ocean because its body filters and pumps out excess salt. Freshwater fish lack this salt-pumping ability and would die in salt water. Similarly, a saltwater fish might die in fresh water because it doesn't have the ability to pump out excess fresh water that seeps into its cells.

Some species can readily move between fresh and salt water at will. Fish with a lower tolerance for change can move from fresh or salt water into brackish areas, but no further. Many times you will find fish right at the interface where freshwater mixes with salt. The mouth of a small river or coastal stream is an excellent place to fish a streamer fly.

Water Color

The color of water will impact how you fish a given lake or stream. In crystal-clear, slow-moving water, for example, a fish will have a long time to inspect your fly prior to making its eat or no-eat decision. Here you may have to use fine tippets, and you may even have to take advantage of fluorocarbon's ability to disappear under water. When water takes on more color—when terrestrial runoff leaches through forests of decaying leaves, for example—the length and type of your leader becomes less important. Still, fish can distinguish significant detail even under these less-than-ideal conditions. They may not be able to see as far, but if your fly drifts within their window of vision, they will see it. Fish see and react to natural movement extremely well, whereas unnatural movements can send them in the opposite direction, pronto.

Light

Like you, fish have superb eyesight that allows them to see objects in color. Also, available light plays a big role in the daily activity of fish; many fish use light to find food, while others seek cover during the brightest hours of the day and go out to feed when less light makes them less vulnerable. During low-light times—early morning or soon after sunset—some species become more active near the surface or in shallow water. Perhaps in low light, these otherwise vulnerable areas feel safe. Other species, like striped bass and walleye, have excellent low-light vision, an advantage that makes them successful predators. As an angler, getting out just at dusk or in the very early morning before the sun rises can help you catch some of these wary fish.

There is also some indication that fish may be attracted to the polarized light reflected by certain prey species. There are a number of natural and synthetic materials on the market that copy this polarized reflection.

In most cases, however, fish will detect and home in on fly movement. Fish have a network of nerves along their sides through which they can feel even slight vibrations. It is through this "lateral line" sensor network that the fish can detect the vibrations your fly gives off underwater, regardless of the amount of available light.

TIP: Use dark streamer flies in low-light conditions. On bright days use streamers that match the color of the resident baitfish or prey species.

On sunny days, be aware of your shadow. Fish are skittish when it comes to moving shadows. Keep low, move slow, and try to keep the sun in front of you.

Proximity of Other Fish

Some fish prefer the security of being close to other fish of the same species. In schools, these fish can feed while relying on a nearby fish to react quickly should a predator make a threatening approach. If one segment of the school is startled, the whole school can react and escape harm. This is one reason why we don't drop a weighted fly right on top of a jittery fish. The sound of the splash may not seem like much to you, but it will probably signify danger to a nervous fish, and off he'll go along with the whole school.

A soft presentation is always preferred, but sometimes when you're using heavier flies a soft presentation is nearly impossible. In these situations, you may have to cast the fly 15 feet or more from the fish you want to catch, and then strip the fly line, carefully drawing your fly near the fish. Hopefully, the fish will spot the movement of your fly and make it its next meal. Another idea is not to cast to the lead fish. Cast to the second or third fish. Should your fly startle that fish, others in the group may continue to follow the unsuspecting lead fish. (For more information about stripping, see "The Strip Set" on page 117 of Hours 12–13, Hooking and Fighting a Fish.)

Cover Type

When it comes to seeking cover, many coastal and inland fish species like to be near structure. Often fish will take on the color of the prevailing cover type. Some fish, including trout and salmon, become dark-colored when they're over dark bottoms or they become silvery over light, sandy bottoms. Other species like summer flounder can take on a mottled look to replicate a similarly mottled bottom. Cover and deceptive coloration are all part of the fish's security system and a good camouflage might even help it capture prey. In general, the more cover a fish has the less it will be seen by a larger predator, and the more likely it will live to see another day. Enticing a fish that's in deep cover to eat your fly can be a great and perhaps frustrating challenge, particularly if the fish is in no-eat mode. Try as you may, but sometimes the fish just won't bite. Mark the spot well; you might have to come back early in the morning or at dusk to get a fair shot at this fellow!

One of the reasons why predatory fish migrate is because their prey migrate as well. If the prey travels hundreds or thousands of miles, the predators will stay right with them. Sometimes the prey will be secure very near the shore, and the predators—when they feel hungry enough—must go in after them. Occasionally, in great panic, the bait will flee in all directions, and they sometimes beach themselves where they become easy pickings for birds and other critters.

While some predators follow their prey, others use the opposite strategy: they find the best spot to wait for their prey to come to them. These ambush sites are at a premium and are vigorously defended, usually by the biggest and most aggressive fish. In most cases, water flow and current patterns will shape these feeding stations, and natural drift will bring a consistent flow of food to the occupant.

Spotting and Fishing Ambush Sites

Watch for places where predators may be laying in wait for prey. They will have consistent surface and subsurface water flow patterns, and the current won't be excessively strong. You can find such places behind rocks, fallen trees, seawalls, groins, and breakwaters. If the fish is feeding from the surface, it will make continual, almost rhythmic feeding forays. The good news, from an angler's perspective, is you have found fish in feeding mode; the bad news is you don't know what it might be feeding on. Before you cast your fly and put the fish in the defensive no-eat mode, spend a moment to try to figure out what's on the fish's menu. Sometimes it's quite obvious; at other times it's not. In either case, figuring out what the fish are eating can be great fun.

Elements That Influence Where Fish Are

Among the influences that can help you determine where to find fish are barometric pressure, wind, water level, and the presence of other organisms such as predators and certain small plankton species.

Barometric Pressure

Many fish species have well-developed internal air bladders that they use for balance and flotation. It's also possible that these bladders can sense sound and changes in barometric pressure. Some anglers swear that fish become more active as barometric pressure decreases prior to a storm. Other anglers may take the opposite position.

The science of this is not well established, so you'll have to decide for yourself whether there is anything to it or not. I've caught a lot of fish on rainy days, and I've caught them on clear days, too. On similar days in other places, I've caught nothing. Nevertheless, if you choose to fish when you know the barometric pressure is dropping, be sure to get off the water as soon as possible if there's a threat of lightning.

Wind

Without a doubt, wind is a big influence on fish activity. In some cases, wind can pick up a lot of terrestrial organisms from trees and grasses and drop them on the water's surface, offering fish a pleasant dietary change from their normal aquatic fare. On the other hand, as wind strength builds, surface waves can decrease the fish's ability to see and recognize potential food organisms. Moreover, your ability to spot fish will decrease as wind increases. Higher wind strength creates even larger waves, and these may stir up the bottom in shallow water. If the waves become large enough, sand and grit become suspended in the water and fish have to endure the potentially abrasive effects of these particles on their gill filaments. Obviously, some species of carp and catfish have adapted quite well to murky conditions, but other fish have not. Most active predators will tolerate only so much of this "foul weather," and if the water becomes so turbid that they can't locate their prey, they're outta there.

Water Level

The high water levels that follow a storm or rapid snow melt usually decrease fish-feeding activity in rivers. When such conditions exist, fish may hug the bottom or find cover where the slower flows don't drain a lot of energy. Finding these pockets and getting your fly into them can be very difficult and your only hope for catching a fish may be to go to a lake or pond, where runoff and currents aren't an issue. Another tactic is to find an inlet where a river or stream dumps into a bay, lake, or pond. Fish will often wait here to take advantage of any food that's being carried in the current.

The Presence of Other Organisms

Plankton blooms impact many fish. Plankton are small, often microscopic plants and animals that live in water. They usually live in a somewhat controlled balance in which no one species becomes overwhelmingly dominant. There are times, however, when conditions become ideal for some plant species, called phytoplankton, to grow exponentially. In such conditions the water will actually turn green, brown, or red, and the blooms create conditions that some fish simply avoid. In some cases, a bloom will block the entrance of a small bay, cove, or estuary, and fish can be trapped within.

Like other plants, phytoplankton produce and release oxygen, which fish need, but only during the daylight hours. During the dark of night, plankton use oxygen. Occasionally, just before dawn, the oxygen level within the bloomed waters becomes so low that large numbers of fish—especially baitfish—die. As soon as the sun rises, the plankton begin to manufacture and release oxygen again. However, it's often too late for the fish, and the stench of dead fish that have washed up on the beach now hangs in the air.

Fish Live in the Water

Yes, obviously fish live in water. But they don't live just anywhere in the water; they tend to be particular about where they hang out. If you can identify the places that appeal to fish, you're more likely to catch them.

There are two main types of water—nonflowing and flowing—and there is a big difference in how you fish each one.

Still Water

Nonflowing water, also known as flat water, is found in lakes, ponds, and bays. Because the water isn't moving much, the fish have a relatively long time to look at your fly before they decide whether it's something worth eating. For this reason, fishing in nonflowing water for selective fish can be most difficult indeed. As a fly angler, you have to use active strategies to entice these fish to bite.

Stealth is also important on flat water. From a fish's perspective, the environment in nonmoving water doesn't change that much or, if it does, it changes very slowly. Since the fish is there every day, it gets to know what should and should not be there. Certainly ducks, beaver, alligators, or other swimming animals will pass through occasionally, and for the most part the fish doesn't feel threatened by these familiar movements. On the other hand, the fish will perceive the unfamiliar movement of an angler plodding into the water or yelling to a buddy as a threat, and it will turn tail and flee.

TIP: When fishing quiet water, move slowly and quietly. If you can, cast your flies so they land with minimum splash. If you're fishing with a dry fly, initially lift the rod tip slowly to avoid making a loud pop as the fly breaks from the water's surface. (See the casting discussion starting on page 59.)

Fly movement is most important. As always, you need to select a fly that successfully mimics a food item that will attract the fish you're seeking. In still water, however, you must then impart movement to the fly. Stripping, or pulling, the fly line in rapid 1- to 2-inch pulses will cause the fly to appear as if it's actively swimming. Perhaps it will look like it's trying to dart out of harm's way, and the fish will follow in hot pursuit. Sometimes a mere short twitch is all you need do to entice a strike. (See Hours 12–13, Hooking and Fighting a Fish for more information about how to fish flies.)

In still water, as elsewhere, most fish like to be near structure. Essentially, structure is anything that's different along a relatively uniform lake, bay, or pond bottom. A sunken tree, log jam, rock pile, or several old tires can be effective fish attractors. Perhaps they give the fish a sense of security or a place to launch an attack on some unsuspecting prey. Certainly,

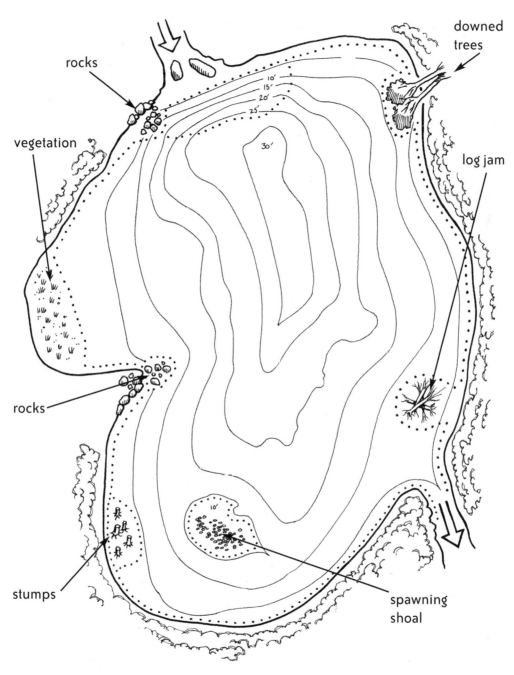

Typical pond showing likely places where fish may be found. The dotted line indicates fish-holding areas.

little fish like structure, as they offer a place to feed as well as a place to hide should a predator attack.

TIP: If you happen to catch a fish near a log jam or brush pile, quickly use the pressure of your rod tip to move the fish away from the structure before it tries to seek cover in it. If your fish gets entangled, you might lose both the fish and your fly.

Drop-offs are great places to look for fish. Fly fishers often find drop-offs by accident as they move about the edge of a lake, suddenly taking that fateful step that sends water over the top of their chest waders. If this happens to you, next time remember where the spot is and fish it from a distance. A wise angler will often probe unfamiliar waters with a wading staff before making a misstep into deeper water.

Fish will often hang just below the rim of a drop-off. I once fished a high mountain lake in Colorado for greenback cutthroat trout. A small stream entered at the far end and formed a drop-off. I was retrieving a smallish fish I had caught back toward the shallow side of the drop-off when a huge trout shot out of the bottom and raced for my fish! It missed, but if I ever get back to that lake again, I'll bring a few big flies that mimic a smaller trout.

Sometimes you'll see a fish cruising just below the surface of still water, rising intermittently as it moves along and encounters something to eat. Your objective here is to try to pattern the fish; that is, anticipate where it will rise next. Select just the right fly and cast it well ahead of the fish but where it's most likely to go. Then wait until the fish gets close to your fly. A slight twitch might be all you need to provoke a strike.

Flowing Water

Slow-moving water can be almost as challenging to fish as the still water of a lake or pond. If fish have a long time to study your presentation,

both areas likely
to hold fish

Deeper, quiet water below riffles is a popular holding spot for fish.

they can be very discerning. This is particularly true of fish that get a lot
of pressure from anglers. They've seen it all—lures, flies, worms, and artificial baits with attractive smells and colors—and will avoid anything that
looks unnatural. It's sometimes effective to fish these waters when the light
is subdued, such as in the early morning, at dusk, or on a dark, cloudy day.
And sometimes fog can be an effective angler ally.

Most anglers like to fish in a moderate flow when the fish are rising to
the surface. Such prime conditions provide the angler with considerable
advantages. First, rising fish are in feeding mode. Second, the fish don't
have a lot of time to decide if something looks natural or not. Third, since
you can see where the fish are rising, you know about where they are. The
fly you use in these situations should closely resemble what the fish
are eating. Take a few moments to study the surface. Can you see what

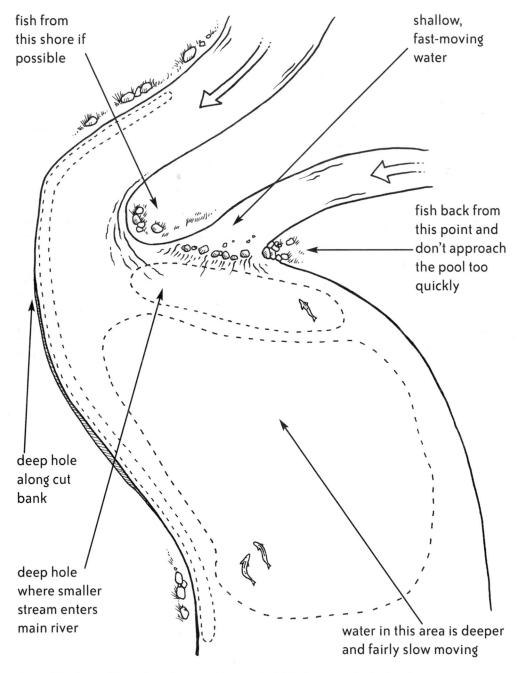

fish from
this shore if
possible

shallow,
fast-moving
water

fish back from
this point and
don't approach
the pool too
quickly

deep hole
along cut
bank

deep hole
where smaller
stream enters
main river

water in this area is deeper
and fairly slow moving

*Areas like these (dotted circles) are likely to hold fish; particularly the deeper water
below riffles.*

This angler is fishing deep holes along the inside bank of the river and has a nice fish on.

they're eating? (See page 105.) Can you catch one of these bugs? If you can't match the color, can you match the shape or size? Usually a fly having two out of three of these characteristics will enable you to catch a few fish. Match all three, and someone might ask you to put on a fly-fishing clinic!

Tip: When you spot a place where a fish is rising, cast 5 or 6 feet upstream of that place. The fish is always looking upstream to see what's coming its way; by casting several yards above the fish, you have time to get your fly line under control (see "Line Control" on page 110) and to make small adjustments to be sure the fly will drift right over the fish. If the fish snubs your presentation, do not lift the fly from the water right away in order to make another presentation.

Wait until it's well downstream of the fish or you get obvious drag on the fly
before lifting it. Remember my grandfather's words: "If you want to catch fish,
you've got to have your hook in the water." By allowing your fly to drift, you
won't frighten the fish you're targeting, and you might have a chance of
catching another fish that you didn't see farther downstream.

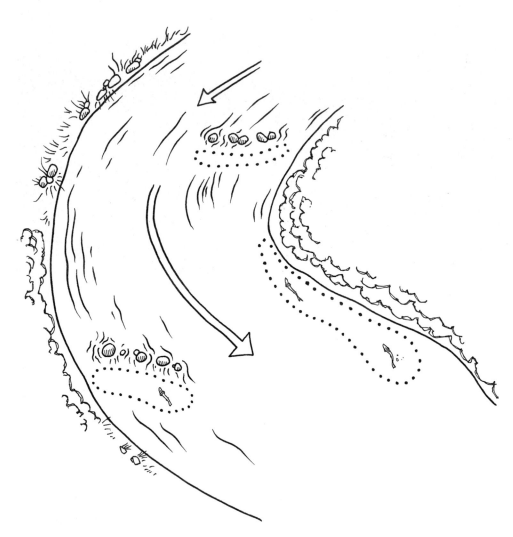

*Eddies behind rocks and sharp bends (shown by dotted circles) are good places to
find fish.*

fish here behind
this riffle

along this seam

small backwaters
like this hold fish

When fishing a river below a confluence, concentrate on a few spots more likely to hold fish. Approach these areas slowly, and then fish upstream. Keep a low profile.

If you spend a little more time reading it, the water's surface will offer several other clues to help you find fish. Look for transitions such as seams and interfaces between fast- and slower-moving water, warm and colder water, shallow and deeper water (drop-offs), or fresh and salt water. You can also find fish in transition areas like inlets and outlets, where the moving water brings food to the fish.

Vegetation, particularly grasses and low shrubs, growing along a stream bank or lakeshore is another type of interface. When the wind blows, terrestrial bugs like beetles, ants, and grasshoppers commonly fall into the water, and an alert fish is rewarded with a meal.

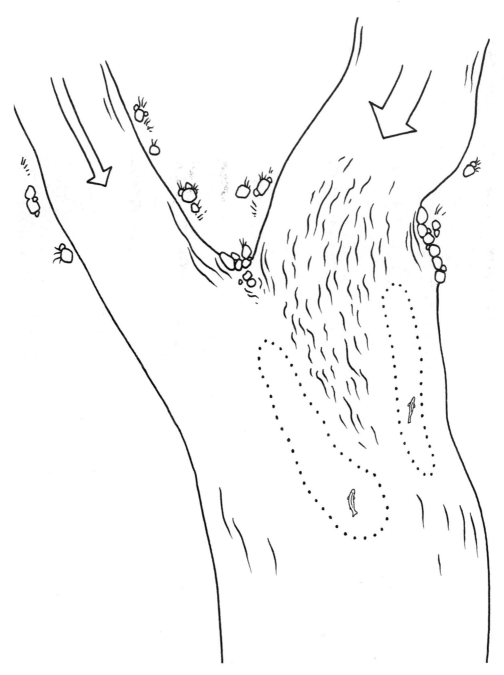

Fish along the edges of chutes just on the interface of fast and slower-moving water.

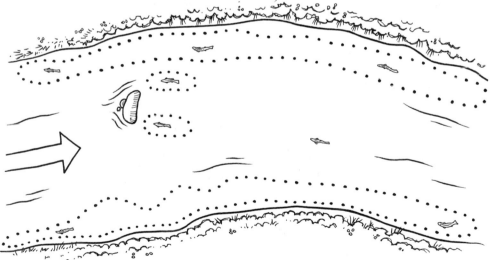

When fishing along grass-lined rivers, you might try dry flies like grasshoppers and beetles—especially if the wind is blowing.

When swift-moving water flows around large rocks, pockets of calmer water form directly behind them. Look for fish in these areas.

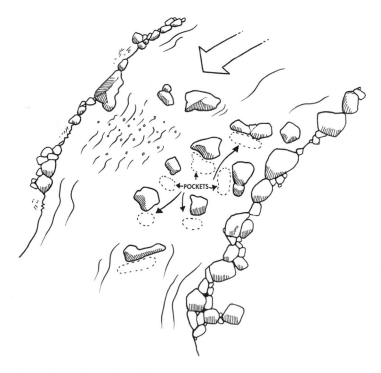

Typical pocket water fishery.

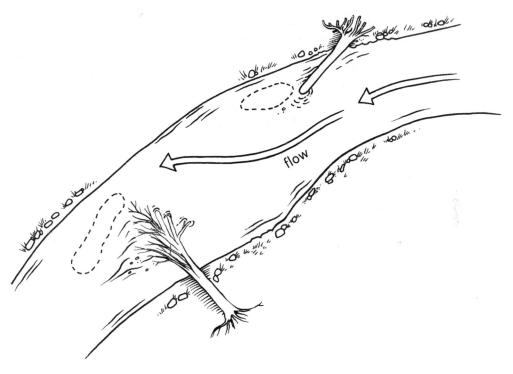

Fish downstream of logs, points, and brush piles.

Look also for any unique water flow patterns such as those around a partially submerged tree or at the outlet of a small river as it enters a bay (see also "Saltwater Fly-Fishing" in Hour 20). Fish are almost always looking for something to eat, and most of these transition areas offer some advantage to the predator. On the downstream side of large rocks you'll find pockets of water that can hold fish, and the plunge pool at the base of a dam is an ideal spot to find fish. Predators can handle turbulence better than their prey, so you'll often find bigger fish feeding in rapidly moving water.

However, if you get to the river and the water is roiling, it's best to find a smaller stream or some flat water to fish. Not only is it dangerous to fish very fast water, it's extremely difficult. If you must fish rough waters, be extremely careful and look for pocket water behind rocks or along the edge of a riverbank. You'll probably need weighted flies to get them down quickly before you get line drag. And whatever you do, stay out of fast-moving water; it can easily sweep you downstream. Instead, fish from the bank.

Time Check

Since we're nearing the end of an hour packed with information, let me summarize a few of the main points of finding and catching fish. The real secret to catching fish is finding a place where the habitat fulfills a fish's needs, preferences, and influences. As an angler, your goal is to insert your fly into the natural relationship that exists between the predator and the prey. If there are few natural prey organisms in the area, predators will likely be somewhere else where they can more readily capture a meal.

Fish have excellent eyesight and hearing, so approach fishing spots stealthily. Once there, figure out what the fish are eating, mimic the size, shape, and color of their food, and deliver the fly to the areas that likely hold fish. Then try to make the fly's movements look as natural as possible. In some cases, the natural insect will be quiet and passive, and a drag-free drift with no movement is appropriate. In other cases, you'll need to strip the fly line to make the fly move in a way that's similar to the natural. (See "The Strip Set" on page 117 of Hours 12–13, Hooking and Fighting a Fish.) In either case, you're actively trying to provoke the fish into striking the fly. Whack! . . . Fish on!

HUR 11

WHAT YOU NEED TO KNOW ABOUT FLIES

There are flies that are tied to impress anglers and there are flies that are tied to catch fish. From my perspective, there are certain flies in the latter group that you must have wherever you go (see "Flies" in the Resources section on page 244). In this chapter I'll introduce you to the freshwater flies I find most useful. Afterward, if you're interested in learning more about saltwater flies, you can refer to the section entitled "Saltwater Fly-Fishing" in Hour 20.

Dry Flies and Wet Flies

There are several categories into which flies fall, and for our purposes I'll focus mainly on two: dry flies and wet flies. *Dry flies* float on the water's surface and are intended to look like floating prey. *Wet flies* sink below the water's surface and are intended to look like small fish or other forms of aquatic life. I'll discuss each of these categories in turn.

Dry Flies

Dry flies mimic the adult forms of insects—their graceful wings, diverse body shapes, and all of the fantastic shades of color and sizes characteristic of bugs that have evolved over the millennia. There are literally thousands of dry-fly patterns. For some of us, dry flies represent the pinnacle of form and quality in the fly-fishing world. The patterns are usually very specific and standardized, such that when you tell other anglers you're using a size 14 Adams, they know exactly what you're talking about.

This happy angler shows off a pretty Arctic grayling he caught on a Black Gnat Parachute dry fly.

There is great diversity in hook sizes, lengths, weight, and shapes. Hook eyes can face upward, downward, or point straight out. Nevertheless, dry flies need to be balanced to float properly, and hook manufacturers have standardized hook sizes and shapes to make this need easier. Further, body materials such as dry-fly hackle,

Seeing What the Fish Sees

Understanding what the fish sees is critical if you want to catch fish, so try to see your dry fly from the fish's perspective. Simply place one of your flies in a clear glass bowl that's partially filled with water. Lift the bowl above you so you can see the fly through the water from underneath. Now ask yourself, "If I were a fish, would I want to eat that?" If the fly doesn't look right or sit right in your bowl of water, it probably won't look right to a fish. As a flytier, you may have to make a few adjustments, such as modify the tail length or use a hackle that's better sized to fit the hook.

which has very little water-absorbing webbing, contribute to a fly's ability to stay afloat. (For more about fly-tying materials, see Hours 21–24, An Introduction to Fly Tying.)

BLACK GNAT PARACHUTE

The most effective dry fly I use is the Black Gnat Parachute (BGP). Fish love it. This fly, like all parachute patterns—patterns in which the hackle is wound horizontally around an upright post—has the uncanny ability of always landing upright, no matter how you toss it. Also, since there are a lot of little black bugs all over the world, the BGP seems to work well just about everywhere I've traveled. You can tie it on a size 14 hook, although you may want to have some 18s and 10s for variety. (See page 215 for tying instructions.)

Black Gnat Parachute.

ELK-HAIR CADDIS

The Elk-Hair Caddis is another dry fly never to be without. Flies with dark brown to very light tan elk hair and olive, brown, rust, gray, or pale yellow body color work well. You can find caddis flies just about anywhere, and from a fish's perspective, the colors I've listed match a considerable number of bugs in its diet. You'll cover many bases if you have different sizes and colors of these flies.

An Elk-Hair Caddis (left) and a variation of a Goddard Caddis.

OTHER DRY FLIES TO CONSIDER

There are several other dry flies worth your consideration. My favorites include the Adams, or Parachute Adams (sizes 12, 14, and 16); any good mayfly pattern, such as March Brown, Quill Gordon, Light Cahill, and Light Hendrickson, in gray, pale yellow, dark brown, or cream (preferably size 14); Humpies, red and yellow (size 12); and Blue-Wing Olives (sizes 16, 18, and 20). For those of you who wish to catch bass and bluegill, try some poppers in various colors (sizes 6 and 8). Finally, ant, beetle, and grasshopper imitations are useful, particularly on windy days when the naturals may be blown into the water from trees, shrubs, or streamside grasses.

Wet Flies

Wet flies are made to sink. In general, the shanks of wet-fly hooks are a bit longer than a standard dry-fly hook. As is true of dry flies, color, shape, and proportion are critical to wet-fly success—match your fly to the natural and you'll likely be rewarded.

This wild rainbow trout was caught on a Bead-Headed Golden Ribbed Hare's Mask Nymph.

Since fish feed underwater most of the time, wet flies are extremely important. The category of wet flies divides very neatly into nymphs and streamers.

NYMPHS

Without a doubt, there are two nymphs to include in every angler's fly box. The first is the Bead-Headed Golden Ribbed Hare's Mask Nymph. I like it in sizes 12–18, although I catch most of my fish on size 14 hooks. This fly is

Bead-Headed Golden Ribbed Hare's Mask Nymph (left) and Pheasant-Tail Nymph.

A Flytier's Look at Insect Transformation

You don't need to learn the scientific name of every insect out there to understand what inspires fly design. However, having a general understanding of how an insect transforms from nymph to adult will help you see the larger picture.

Many female insects deposit their eggs on the water's surface and the eggs sink to the bottom. Later, the eggs hatch into *nymphs*—a consistent source of food for fish. Flytiers know this and have designed all kinds of flies to mimic nymphs.

When the nymph is ready to metamorphose to the next stage of its lifecycle, it may gather or generate a bubble of gas. When the bubble is big enough, the nymph rises to the surface much faster than it might if it were to swim or rise on its own. A rising bug represents an easy meal to a fish, so speed is important.

Once on the surface, the insect must break through the surface film and hatch, or *emerge*, from its outer shell into its adult, avian form. In a perfect world, this process would happen very quickly. But this isn't a perfect world, and some bugs have their problems. Sometimes the shell, also called a shuck, doesn't fully break open, or its wings don't fully open to their usable form. When situations like these happen, the bug is at an ever-increasing risk of becoming fish food—hence the development of flies called *emergers*.

great for bass, crappie, bluegill, and trout. The fly just seems to say, "Come on, fish, bite me!" (See page 225 for tying instructions.)

Insects have three distinct segments: head, thorax, and abdomen. When I tie this pattern, I put a bit of Hare's Mask Plus in the thorax of the fly. Hare's Mask Plus contains a small amount of shredded pearlescent Mylar material blended with the guard hairs from the face of the rabbit, otherwise called a hare's mask. The Mylar gives the fly a small amount of attractive flash. With a gold, silver, or black bead to increase its sink rate, this fly becomes a real killer. If you are initially going to purchase some flies, ask the shop keeper if he has any nymphs tied with Hare's Mask Plus.

The Pheasant-Tail Nymph is another must-have. I prefer this versatile nymph in smaller sizes, from 16 through 20. Bead-headed versions are also a must.

STREAMERS

Streamers are flies that imitate bait-fish, crustaceans, or aquatic inverte-brates. They are usually fished with a great deal of action (i.e., stripping) and often catch the largest fish.

When it comes to streamers, there is but one fly that you absolutely must have. The Woolly Bugger is, in my opinion, the most effective fly ever designed. This pattern and its variants arguably catch more fish for more anglers than all other flies combined.

Woolly Bugger.

The bead-headed versions don't seem to improve the sink rate or change the overall effectiveness of the fly, so when I tie the fly I simply wrap a weighted wire around the hook shank before covering it with a layer of chenille. For those of you who don't want to use lead wire, Gudebrod Inc. makes a tin alloy wire that's more environmentally friendly.

Chenille comes in lots of colors, so go to a nearby tackle shop or a millinery or craft shop and play around with creating your own color combinations. Black and olive Woolly Buggers are effective, as are those made with teal chenille, an olive marabou tail, and a black palmered hackle. To finish this fly, try building a big head with some extra wraps of bright-red thread.

EMERGERS

Emergers are insects in the process of metamorphosing from aquatic infancy to avian adulthood. This change is critical and often difficult. The nymph must reach the water's surface, break out of its *shuck*, a shell-like structure, and emerge as a flying insect. Timing is crucial, as every fish and every bird wants to get an easy meal. Even bats are known to feed on insects emerging from the water at night. A successful fly imitates an insect struggling to get out of its aquatic shell at the surface. These are not dry or wet flies, per se, but rather they have characteristics of both; emergers are fished partially above and partially below the water's surface.

The CDC Emerger is a must-have emerger fly, and it's effective in sizes 18–28. (See page 221 for tying instructions.) CDC is short for *Cul de Cunard* and specifically refers to specialized feathers surrounding the oil gland on ducks and other waterfowl. These feathers hold the oil that birds use to preen themselves, making their feathers waterproof. Without the oil, waterfowl would become very wet, or possibly even sink.

CDC Emerger.

Some clever angler figured out a way to use these feathers to make a fly—the CDC Emerger—that partially floats and partially sinks. It perfectly mimics an insect that, having just emerged onto the water's surface following its nymph phase, is trying to free itself from its underwater shell and become airborne.

ATTRACTOR PATTERNS

From time to time you'll hear the term *attractor pattern*. Also known as search patterns, attractor patterns are often very colorful or somewhat larger flies that

In this close-up view of a CDC feather you can see the fine oil-holding bristles that extend off the side of the branching fibers.

really don't look much like any bug, fish, or other organism that's common to the stream or lake you're fishing. But because they look so different they can provoke fish and induce a strike, and they can be very useful when the fishing is slow. Some very popular attractor flies include red or yellow Humpy, Royal Wulff, and Spruce streamers. Many other streamer flies and perhaps even the Woolly Bugger may be used as a search pattern.

Selecting the Right Fly

Now that you know something about the different varieties of flies, how do you know which fly to tie onto your leader?

You may have heard the adage that 10 percent of the anglers catch 90 percent of the fish. A fly-fishing corollary is that, in all likelihood, the most successful fly fishers use fewer than a dozen fly patterns to catch most of their fish. They all seem to have a "go-to" fly or two that they use when they really want to catch a fish. They put a lot of confidence in these flies and really know how to present and fish them. If you can simplify your own approach this way, you'll catch fish and build a significant level of fishing confidence and experience using only a few critical patterns in various sizes.

TIP: Ask experienced anglers what their "go-to" fly patterns are and how they fish them. Most anglers will share this information while they're suiting up or when they're putting things away at the end of the day. Try not to ask while they're actually fishing, unless they initiate the conversation. It's important to respect a fellow fisher's right to peace and quiet.

In most cases, fish are not as selective as they're often portrayed. Sure, there are times when you better have the absolute correct pattern, especially if you're fishing for trout. Most of the time, however, if you merely try to match the size, color, and shape of whatever the fish are eating you'll catch some fish. Therefore, one of the first things you must learn is to tailor your fly to the fish you want to catch. Fish are out there eating things day in and day out. Their diet, however, does change from time to time, and the most successful anglers are able to modify their presentations to emulate more closely what the fish may be eating at any given moment. In fly-angling terms this is often called *matching the hatch*. Although the term suggests matching an insect hatch, it pertains to all things that fish eat: insects, smaller fish, shrimp, crabs, mulberries, and anything else that whets a fish's appetite. If the fish are eating small things, you have to use small flies. Conversely, if the fish are preying on larger critters, you have to go big. Get this right, and you're well on your way to catching a lot of fish!

Finding Information

So, how do you go about finding out what the fish are eating, and what do you look for? Answering these questions is not always easy, but here are several ideas and resources that will help you get started.

If you're fishing for trout, many locations or river systems produce hatch tables or charts that, based on extensive experience of entomologists and anglers, predict which insects will be hatching during a given time frame. These tables often include a list of fly patterns and fly sizes that will help you become oriented more quickly to the body of water where you'll be fishing. Usually you can obtain a copy of this information from the local chapter of Trout Unlimited or Federation of Fly Fishermen or your nearest tackle shop.

ONLINE RESEARCH

Doing online research can often yield good results. You can search for hatch tables that have been produced for the river or other body of water you'll be fishing, or you can see if doing a search for the body of water itself yields any fishing information.

EXPERIENCED FISHERS

You can always go to your tackle shop and ask someone who fishes all the time. Or better yet, spend a day fishing with a professional guide. Although this may cost some money, a good guide can teach you more in a few hours than you could possibly learn in a week or two by yourself.

Hatch Tables

INSECT	JAN.	FEB.	MAR.	APR.	MAY	JUNE	JULY	AUG.	SEPT.	OCT.	NOV.	DEC.	SUGGESTED PATTERN
Blue-Wing Olive (BWO)			X	X	X					X	X	X	Dry: BWO, Parachute BWO, Parachute Adams; Nymphs: Pheasant-Tail, Hare's Mask, BWO emergers (12–18)
Pale Morning Dun (PMD)					X	X	X	X					Dry: PMD, PMD Parachute, Light Cahill; Nymphs: Pheasant-Tail, Hare's Mask, PMD emergers (14)
Tricos						X	X	X	X				Trico Spinner, Adams (18–20)
Mosquito					X	X	X	X					Mosquito patterns (18)
Caddis			X	X	X	X	X	X	X	X	X		Dry: Elk-Hair Caddis, Light- and Dark-Wing; Caddis nymphs (14–18)
Ants				X	X	X	X	X	X	X			Black Ant, Foam Ant, CDC Ant (14–16)
Beetles						X	X	X	X				Deer-Hair Beetle (14–16), Foam Beetle (14–16)
Grasshoppers							X	X	X	X			Joe's Hopper (6), Foam Hopper (6)
Scuds	X	X	X	X	X	X	X	X	X	X	X	X	Olive Scud patterns (18)
Midges	X	X	X	X	X	X	X	X	X	X	X	X	Griffith's Gnat (20), Midge patterns (20–22)

Note: The above table is a hypothetical hatch chart, typical of what one might find for a given river system. Charts may not always give the size range of the patterns you might encounter, so you may need to ask someone at the local fly shop if he or she has current information.

Remember, the best guides are out there fishing every day, so they really build an extensive catalog of experience. (See Hour 18 for more information about fishing with a guide.)

WATCH THE FISH YOURSELF

There are fly anglers who will tell you that the best way to find out what fish are eating is to go to the water and figure it out for yourself. By doing this you'll use every observational skill you have, and with time you'll develop enhanced abilities to see things that others will miss. Be patient, and look.

TIP: On a bright, sunny day, bronze-tinted polarized sunglasses will reduce the glare and allow you to see what's going on under the water's surface.

Some anglers will just sit for a while and watch the water when they first arrive at their fishing spot, even before they tie on their first fly. When he was a youngster, my buddy was driven nuts by his father's "ritual" of watching the water. My buddy wanted to fish . . . not watch. His father's patience was rewarded, however, when he would finally take out the fly-tying vise and custom tie a fly right there. The boy would tie the fly onto his leader and invariably, smack! Fish on!

What was his father looking for? He most likely was looking for the specific size, color, and shape of the bug that the fish were rising to eat. Several types and sizes of insects can be hatching at any given moment, and the fish may seem to be eating only one type. The key is to watch fish eat and note what they're eating and how.

As you become more skilled—and perhaps go over the deep end with your enthusiasm for fly-fishing—you may even want to buy a pump specifically designed to evacuate the contents of a fish's stomach for closer examination.

Keep in mind that "flies" are not the only eaters on a fish's menu. There are myriad other fly patterns that are available on the market. There are flies that look like certain marine worms, which are particularly effective when the worms are mating. Other flies look like crustaceans, snails, ants, beetles, grasshoppers, or mice. If a critter is part of a fish's diet, you can be sure that someone has designed a fly to represent it. Most flies have a characteristic shape and color and are made to imitate or match natural organisms.

How to Read What the Fish Are Doing

Go to a place that has a healthy fish population. If you're not sure where such a place is, ask your state district fishery biologist. Once there, think like an artist and look at the detail on the water's surface. Was the water dancing differently when you first arrived? Was that a swirl? Was that a flash? Was the fish's rise a violent surface burst (in which case you would try your dry-fly imitation) or just a soft slurp (in which case you would try your emerger)? Exactly where did the fish rise, and how often does it come up? All of these observations can provide clues to how to catch fish.

Are you seeing insects rising from the surface but no fish splashes? If so, you can assume that the fish are feeding under water. In fact, fish feed under water about 90 percent of the time, so you may have to go deep with your fly to get them. Try a bead-head nymph or a Woolly Bugger.

What do you do when you arrive at a place where there is a known fish population, but you don't see a thing . . . not even a flash? The water is calm and stays that way. Not even a bubble rises to give you a hint that the fish are eating on the surface. Again, you can assume the fish are feeding under water. In this case, you might want to use attractor or search patterns. If one pattern doesn't work after a reasonable effort, either move on to another spot or try another pattern.

To complete your presentation after you cast the fly, you may even need to provoke a strike by enhancing fly movement. And this subject, my friends, is just one part of catching fish that we'll take a look at in the next chapter.

H⊕URS 12–13

HOOKING AND FIGHTING A FISH

Before we get into fishing tactics, let's talk fish. For the most part, there are two kinds of animals: grazers and predators. Most of the fish you'll be pursuing are predators. Most predators are influenced by two forces: fear and greed. From a fish's perspective, it wants to eat as much as possible without getting eaten itself.

It's amazing how much a greedy fish will stuff into its gut. Anglers have reported seeing as many as three full-size trout crammed into the stomach of a very large brown trout. Largemouth bass are known to be especially gluttonous. And I have witnessed the ultimate gluttony in bluefish, a saltwater predator known for its savagery, who after gorging as much as possible, regurgitates everything and then resumes killing and eating once again. But remember: as distasteful as the behavior may seem, these predator-prey relationships are natural and have evolved over the millennia to keep populations from expanding uncontrollably.

So how can we use this information to help us catch fish? As an angler, this part of your job will be easy. Fish want to eat. The big "but," as I mentioned earlier, is that fish also do not want to be eaten . . . or caught. Thus there is the fear factor. Through the ages, fish have developed a healthy fear of birds and other animals. Great blue heron, kingfishers, ospreys, eagles, cormorants, mergansers, and terns chase them relentlessly. Otter, mink, seals, and other mammals also eat their fair share of fish. And most of all—although perhaps unseen by most of us—fish eat other fish. Fish catch other fish by employing one of two strategies: they either chase fish or they ambush them.

If we fly fishers are going after the chasers, we need a fly that's worthy of the chase. It should look a lot like and be about the same size as the fish's prey animal. Although streamer flies vary greatly, most were designed to look like fish. To be effective, they also need to move like fish, ideally a disoriented or wounded fish. Predators love to chase the weak and infirm!

Some predators are especially lazy and do not like to expend more energy feeding than they absolutely have to. These fish are the ambushers. They will find a promising spot to hide and will patiently wait for unsuspecting prey to come along. Ambushers are usually less discriminating than chasers, so fly selection is somewhat less important. The real trick to catching ambushers is to find those likely ambush spots.

The same general principle works with fish that eat bugs, leeches, and other smaller prey organisms. You first try to figure out what they're eating, and then you deliver a fly that has similar characteristics to the spot where the fish is likely to be. That said, let's go to the next step.

Line Control

Let's say you've located the fish, have the correct equipment, tied on the right fly, and made the perfect cast. The fish takes the fly, but did you hook the fish? If you use line control, you'll certainly increase your chances. So what is line control? Let me explain the process.

The angler casts straight across the current. (Here, the current flows from the bottom of the photo to the top.)

Then the angler makes an upstream mend, or loop, in the fly line to increase the time before the current pulls the line tight and the fly drags unnaturally against the water flow. That unnatural movement is a tip off to wary fish.

1. As soon as the fly hits flowing water, make your *mend*. Mending is a form of line control that prevents immediate drag from being imposed on the fly by the current's action on the fly line. Essentially, after the fly lands on flowing water, you throw an upstream arc into the fly line. The arc will take a few extra seconds to straighten out and then bow in the downstream direction. During that time, your fly will be carried downstream at the same rate as other things floating around it. Without an upstream mend, the current will drag your fly downstream, and the fly will float at an unnatural speed, which usually is a big turnoff for feeding fish.

2. After you make your mend, use your noncasting hand to quickly achieve line control. Grasp the fly line between the reel and the first stripping guide and place it between the middle and ring fingers of your casting hand. Your purpose here is to recover any line slack that may exist between you and your fly. If you don't take in the slack you won't be able to feel the fish's bite or set the hook.

Use your noncasting hand to recover slack after you've made your upstream mend.

A Closer Look at Line Drag and the Upstream Mend

The water in a river flows at different rates depending on the bottom and the proximity to the river channel. A shallow bottom will add friction to water flow and thus slow it down, while water in a deeper channel flows at a faster rate. As you cast across the river, the water flow will pull, or drag, the floating line at different rates depending on where it lies on the water. The upstream mend gives your fly a slightly longer drag-free drift. This works because, during the time it takes for the upstream arc of line to straighten out, your fly is moving at the same rate as the current; the fly line isn't dragging the fly along and, to the fish, the fly appears to be floating at a natural speed.

You won't catch many fish without line control, even though they may consistently take your fly. Sometimes after making a beautiful presentation upstream with a dry fly, I get so preoccupied with watching the fly that I forget to take in the slack fly line that's created as the fly floats downstream toward me. With all that loose line there is no way I can set the hook when the fish strikes, before it spits out the fly. Learn and practice effective line control, and you'll be well on your way to becoming a competent angler.

Fishing the Fly

Many anglers enjoy watching fish rise to their dry fly. Admittedly, it is quite a thrill to see the drama of the hunt unfold before your eyes as a beautiful fish rises with explosive force to snap your fly from the water's surface. Remember, however, that most of the time fish feed underwater so you must also learn to fish wet flies. Indeed, successful anglers catch more fish by using flies that go down to where the fish are feeding. Consequently we'll focus on both dry flies and wet flies, and the first fact is that you fish each type differently.

TIP: While fishing, get in the habit of checking your flies frequently and removing any grass, algae, or leaf fragments they may have picked up. Also make sure the tail feathers aren't wrapped around the hook bend. A fish will notice a feather—even just one or two fibers—that's wrapped around the bend, deem the fly unnatural, and pass it by. It's especially critical to frequently check your flies when you're fishing in places where the fishing pressure is high. If a fish sees an unnatural fly often enough, it will soon learn to avoid the pattern.

Dry-Fly Fishing

Dry-fly fishing is popular because you see the action happen right before your eyes; if you focus on your fly as it drifts downstream, you may well be rewarded with one of the greatest honors bestowed upon an angler: a fish explosively attacking your fly. Whether you've played the game by tying fur, feathers, and other materials on a hook or by using a store-bought fly, you have fooled your quarry. And it all happened right there for all to see. It's so simple, yet so powerful!

Here are three dry-fly fishing techniques you can try.

THE TIP SET

Perhaps you're wondering how to set the hook. You do what's called the *tip set*.

1. When you know a fish has your fly, raise the rod tip with the same vigor you would use to initiate a back cast. By the time the rod tip reaches the 10 o'clock position, you'll feel the resistance created by the fish and you can stop your rearward motion.

2. If you don't feel the resistance (i.e., if you haven't hooked the fish), snap-stop the rod tip at 1 o'clock, allow the backcast to unfurl behind you, and then recast the fly to within inches of where the fish struck. The fly will be off the water for just a second or two.

Sometimes as the fish returns to the protective depths of the water, it will look back at the surface to see if the fly is gone or if it's still sitting on the same spot. Occasionally, the fish will make another strike. Having already done a tip set with good line control, you have measured the exact distance you need to cast. You merely have to recast and point the rod tip above the spot where you want the fly to land, and you'll hit the mark. Amazing how it works! Try it.

TWITCHING THE FLY

On slow or still water, try casting your fly and letting it sit for ten seconds or so. After the pause, move your rod tip slightly so the fly twitches, or makes a couple of 1- or 2-inch strides across the water's surface. Caddis fly naturals really like to skid along the water, so moving flies that represent them in this way makes sense. Twitching will often provoke a strike.

TIP: If you can see the fish or know about where it is, wait until your fly is within a foot of its nose before twitching it. More than once, I have caught very selective fish using this technique.

Now let's imagine how this technique looks from the fish's point of view. After an insect nymph rises to the water's surface where it changes into a flying bug, or after a land bug accidentally falls into the water, there is a short time during which the bug appears to be in shock and makes very few movements, if any at all. This may be how the fish views the pause just after you cast your fly. Then, as you begin twitching your fly, instinct tells the fish that the fallen insect has regained its composure—or an emerger has prepared its wings for flight—and the fish responds to the movement with a strike.

Fish see this kind of insect behavior every day and recognize it as a familiar pattern. Without processing what it's seeing to any great extent, the fish instinctively decides that if it hesitates to grab the fly, it will lose a meal. To the fish, the twitching action may represent the last split second that a meal is still possible.

Dry-Fly Floatant

Before you subject your dry flies to the world of water, coat them with some dry-fly floatant. My favorite is a white silicone grease sold by Scientific Angler. This stuff really repels water and allows the fly to float high, just as real insects do, despite repeated dunkings. Fish slime will reduce a fly's ability to float, so between landing several big ones, you may have to wash and dry the fly before applying a bit more floatant. Making false casts will air-dry a fly quickly. False casts are overhead casts you make without actually dropping the line into the water. (See Advanced Casting Techniques on page 153.) You can also press the fly onto the sleeve of your shirt or a small piece of chamois to wring out any extra moisture before greasing it up again.

RETRIEVE IT LIKE A WET FLY

Try fishing your dry flies downstream, dry, and then back upstream, wet. Normally dry-fly anglers fish them dry, casting upstream and across the water. During the last part of the float, the fly will pick up speed as the current increases drag on the fly line, causing the fly to swing back toward your side of the river. When the line draws tight, the fly may sink. Now it's a wet fly, and you can retrieve it with the same 1- to 2-inch stripping motions you would use to retrieve wet flies (see "The Strip Set," below). Also, recovering any additional line you may be shooting in this way allows you to align the black mark that designates thirty feet with the rod tip in preparation for your next cast. Moreover, you'll be surprised at how many additional fish you catch using this technique. Many fish do not want to pass up an easy lunch, and when something like your wet dry fly pulls away from them, they may figure it *has* to be good to eat.

TIP: If you can't see your dry fly on the water's surface, then retrieve it as you would a wet fly: point your rod downstream low to the water, and use short but rapid strips. If you get some hits but don't seem to catch the fish, thrust the rod tip a foot or so back downstream and let the fly float right into the mouth of the pursuing fish. It's a nasty trick, but sometimes it works!

Wet-Fly Fishing

Now let's talk about fishing wet flies. The main difference between how you fish a wet fly and how you fish a dry fly is this: when fishing a dry fly you raise the rod tip to set the hook; when fishing a wet fly you must use a strip set, a process in which you set the hook with your noncasting hand by stripping, or pulling, the fly line.

THE STRIP SET

Strip setting moves the fly forward the length of your strip, yet keeps the fly at the same depth as the fish. Even if you don't set the hook, the fish can easily continue the chase and often will. If, however, you raise the tip of your rod prior to hooking the fish, you'll draw the fly too close to the water's surface and away from the interested fish.

A strip set is easy to do. Here's how:

1. Cast your wet fly upstream and across the water. As soon as the fly touches the water, do your upstream mend to prevent immediate, unnatural drag on the fly. Next, gain line control by gathering in any extra slack in the fly line. With your noncasting hand, pinch the fly line to the rod handle, below the first stripping guide.
2. As the fly heads downstream, more slack in the fly line will be created. You can control much of this extra slack by merely lifting the rod tip and then lowering it as the fly passes downstream. To prolong your drag-free drift for a few extra feet, extend your rod hand and the rod tip downstream.

3. Throughout the float, your non-casting hand should be tightly grasping the fly line and be poised to make a sharp 4- to 6-inch pull—the strip set—if you detect any strange fly line movement or tap near and about the fly, caused by an investigating fish. Often these movements or taps will be very subtle, and that's why line control is so critical. If the line is too loose, you won't even feel a hard strike. By the time you react to a bite, your fish will have spit out the fly and be long gone.

The forefinger of the casting hand pinches the fly line against the handle, while the noncasting hand is poised to pull the line in a strip set.

TIP: You can modify your stripping sequence by varying the pulls from between 1 and 3 inches or by using some other pattern that you find catches fish.

4. If you haven't felt a strike by the time your fly reaches directly downstream, you can strip the fly back upstream in a series of short motions. Use your noncasting hand, and make the pulls in rapid succession. To the fish, the jerking fly might look like an insect trying to escape becoming a meal.

The angler sets the hook by drawing the fly line sharply downward about 6 inches. Throughout the process, he continues to loosely pinch the line against the handle with his casting hand.

Don't despair if your fly reaches the end of the line without any fish. When you strip the line back upstream, a fish may be attracted to the motion of the fly. Notice how this angler holds the line in his noncasting hand as he strips.

When the line draws tight and the wet fly nears the furthest point on its downstream drift, the fly will be pulled toward the surface while also swinging toward your side of the river. Strikes often occur during this time. The fly's upward trajectory mimics a nymph rising from the bottom to begin its avian life.

FISHING A WOOLLY BUGGER

I like to fish Woolly Buggers early in the season, especially on lakes and ponds stocked with trout.

At this time of year, when the water is cold, fish stay in deeper water. To get the fly down to them, use a sinking tip fly line. After casting, wait a few seconds before stripping the fly back. Hold the rod tip at or just above the water's surface and make a series of rapid 2-inch strips.

If you feel a bite, continue your stripping sequence until you know you've set the hook. Only when you're *absolutely sure* the fish is hooked do you raise your rod tip to fight the fish (see "Fighting a Fish," page 122).

FISHING A TANDEM RIG

The tandem rig is another technique you can use with a Woolly Bugger. First tie an attractor pattern onto your leader. I recommend using an attractor that's slightly smaller than your Woolly Bugger. Then tie on your Woolly Bugger about 18 inches behind the attractor pattern. Having an attractor pattern in front of your Woolly Bugger can make a big difference in the number of strikes and fish you catch. For attractor patterns, I would use a red and yellow Mickey Finn where there are likely to be brook trout or a Hornberg where there are more brown trout.

To connect the Woolly Bugger to the attractor fly, simply take about 22 inches of tippet material that's the same size or one size smaller than the terminal part of your leader. Tie a small four-twist loop (see page 48 for instructions) at one end and tie on the Woolly Bugger at the other end. Then tie a simple lanyard loop (see page 50 for instructions) to secure the four-twist loop to the bend of the attractor fly hook.

TIP: Tandem rigs may not be legal in all states. Some states allow fishers to use only one hook. Before you tie a tandem rig, be sure to check the fishing regulations of the state in which you're fishing.

Try to visualize how a fish might see a tandem rig like this, and you may get a sense of why it catches fish so successfully. Remember, a fish is like a binary switch, it either wants to eat or it doesn't. As an angler, your job is to entice the fish to eat and, in particular, to want to eat your fly. If the fish is in a "no-eat" mode, you have to evoke an eat response. Now, imagine your attractor fly passing by the fish in 2-inch spurts, followed by your Woolly Bugger in hot pursuit. In the fish's view, the Woolly Bugger wants to eat the attractor fly. This evokes the fish's instinctive drive to eat, and it wants to get in on the action. Rather than go for the smaller attractor fly, however, it presses its attention on the larger and more calorically valuable Woolly Bugger.

Is it more difficult to cast tandem flies? Although it may seem to be a bit more difficult, it really isn't. The secret is to make tight loops with the fly line and try to keep your elbow on a horizontal plane (see "Other Casting Techniques" in Hour 17, page 159). By going back to your casting basics, you'll avoid most tangles.

TIP: When casting two flies, always have your larger, heavier fly be the second or terminal fly. Also, if you see a small tangle, stop casting and untie the mess. It will only get worse if you ignore it.

FISHING A CDC EMERGER

Emerger flies are not quite wet flies and not quite dry flies, and they're effective because they have characteristics of both types of fly. When you see fish sucking the water's surface as opposed to more violently attacking insects riding high above the surface film, think emerger.

When you fish emergers—in this case the CDC Emerger—remember that you want half the fly to be below the water's surface and the other half, supported by the oily CDC feathers, poking just above the surface. From a fish's view, the puffed-up CDC feathers resemble newly emerged wings. The fish has certainly seen such a sight before, and when it sees something that represents food in this way . . . time to eat!

A slight twitch at the right moment can provoke the strike of more finicky fish. You can also drag the fly in 2- to 4-inch strips either underwater or back upstream. The fish will thus perceive your fly as a bug that's almost out of its shuck and having a bit of trouble flying away. And you better get ready because, if you made a good cast, did your upstream mend, and have good line control, it's going to happen . . . Wham! Fish on!

Fighting a Fish

Now that you have hooked a fish, you must somehow bring it to the net. The first thing to do when you're sure a fish is on your hook is raise the rod tip and press the fly line against the rod handle with the fingers of your rod hand. This is a temporary brake. Your objective here is to keep tension on the fly line.

This angler keeps the rod tip high to maintain pressure on the fish. Note that with smaller fish you may not need to retrieve the line onto the reel.

Now you need to control the loose fly line that you stripped in. I often see anglers with expensive reels that have fancy drag systems continue to strip in the fly line after the fish is hooked, in an effort to land the fish. I do not at all recommend this technique. Stripping line may work if the fish is small; however, if you have hooked a really nice fish you can be sure that Murphy's Law will be working against you. Invariably the fish will take a second run, and as sure as you're standing there, the long length of loose fly line floating about will foul around your feet, a branch, or otherwise form a self-tied knot that won't easily pass through your stripping guide . . . and then SNAP goes your tippet and your fish. Since you spent all that extra money on a halfway decent fly reel with some kind of adjustable drag, use it.

Simply put: get it onto the reel as quickly as you can. Turn the handle as fast. If the fish pulls, let some line slip through your line pinch to the fish. All the while, you must maintain a taut line between you and the fish.

Once you have the extra line under control and on the reel, your drag will provide enough resistance to the fish without reaching a point where your tippet breaks. It's OK if the fish takes line, even if it takes you into your backing. That's why you have backing. Further, as more line goes out to the fish, the added burden of pulling all that line through the water acts as an additional drag that will help tire the fish. Soon the fish will stop and give you an opportunity to retrieve the line back onto the reel. Some great fish will take you into your backing three or more times. Now this is fun! With the fly line on the reel, you can really enjoy the fight of the fish. The reel's drag system will apply constant pressure and—when necessary—will give line to the fish to reduce the chances of breaking the tippet.

Getting all that line back onto the reel isn't always easy. For example, if the fish starts to swim toward you, be sure to maintain tension on the line. If you lose tension the fish will invariably shake the hook, and off he'll go.

So how do you keep the line between you and the fish tight and under control while retrieving the loose fly line? Sometimes your only reasonable option, initially, is to strip more line. Also, you can walk backward to put distance between you and the fish. Or you can release a bit more line to the fish if it begins swimming away from you. In some cases, you may need to use all three techniques. With practice, you'll determine which works best for you.

Here's another technique you can try. With your noncasting hand, bring up the slack line and drape it over the pinky of your casting hand so it hangs between your pinky and ring finger. This trick puts some tension on the fly line as it go onto the reel and helps keep the line organized. If this technique is too challenging, simply crank the extra line back onto the reel as fast as you can.

When all the slack between the reel and the fish is gone, release your temporary finger brake, settle in, and enjoy the battle. With the fish on, your key objectives are to keep your rod tip high and to maintain a tight line between you and the fish. Allow the rod's flexibility and the reel's drag to assist you in landing the fish. You don't want that fish to slip the hook and get away.

This angler is fighting a big salmon. Notice how he leans away from the fish and applies sideward rod pressure.

If you've hooked a really big fish, you may want to try this trick: while applying upward pressure with the rod tip, add a bit of sideward pressure on the fish by bringing the rod to a more horizontal position.

Netting a fish is an important skill to learn. If you reach out with the net too soon, you'll spook the fish and it may very well break off. Instead, wait until the fish has a noticeable degree of fatigue before bringing it to the net. Try to sweep the fish over the top of a submerged net and then quickly lift the net. Netting a fish is somewhat easier said than done, but with practice you should get it right more often than not. Here's the key: keep tension on the hook by raising the rod tip as you prepare to net the fish.

A big fish trying to avoid the net can sometimes be so fast and powerful it will actually turn the angler around.

Netting big fish can be like a Three Stooges fire drill. Large wild fish really want to avoid being caught, and they will fight with great endurance to stay out of a net. If they see the net coming, they will swiftly and with enormous power move in another direction. When trying to land such a fish, position the net behind the fish and aggressively sweep it forward, capturing the tail first and then the head. Once again, keep tension on the hook by holding the rod tip high.

Keep the net's rim away from the tippet until the hook gets into the net. Just touching the line above the hook might break off the fish. When netting a fish that's moving vigorously in multiple directions, keeping the rim away from the tippet is often difficult to do. Sometimes you have to guess which way the fish is likely to go and then aggressively move the net toward the fish. Again, if you can, come up from the rear of the fish, which helps keep the net's rim away from the tippet until the fish is secure in the net.

If you're holding the net for a fellow angler and you miss capturing the fish, back off a bit and let the angler try to bring it around once again for a second or third try. Remember, success is assured by swiftly moving the net to the fish. Many a fish have been lost due to timid netting technique or trying to net the fish too soon.

Landing the fish is supposed to be fun, so relax and enjoy the experience. Sometimes it can be a lot of work to get that really big fish in, but I've never heard anyone complain about it the next day. Sure, you may have earned an ache or pain or maybe nursed a small cut or blister—I'm talking really big fish here—but you have had an experience of a lifetime, and now you have a story to tell!

TIP: Be sure to wet your hands and net before handling a trout. Trout have a layer of protective slime on their bodies, and any contact with a dry hand or net can remove it. Without the slime, trout are susceptible to disease and infection.

TIP: To remove the hook from a smaller fish without using a landing net, turn the fish upside down. This often has the effect of quelling the fish long enough for you to get a firm grasp on the hook and make a quick release. If you can keep the fish in the water throughout this process, so much the better.

Time Check

At this point, we're more than halfway there! I hope you're as pleased with your progress as I am. We've been through a lot of critical information, and the pace has been fast. Hopefully you're enjoying the process, as I know you'll enjoy the fishing.

Just to give you some perspective on how well things are going, here's a list of some of the things you've learned so far.

▸ General information about fly-fishing
▸ Fly tackle and accessory equipment
▸ Some useful knots and how to tie them
▸ How to put your fly-fishing equipment together
▸ Casting techniques and how to present a fly
▸ Fly selection
▸ How to catch a fish

The rest of the book is devoted to improving your new skills.

HUR 14

CATCH-AND-RELEASE
TECHNIQUES

As a certified fishery scientist, I know that the 24-hour hooking mortality rate is much lower for fish caught with artificial flies than for fish caught on a lure or baited hook. Why? Generally, flies hook fish in and around the mouth. The mouth area doesn't have any vital organs that would lead to a mortal wound if hooked. Consequently, if you're going to practice catch-and-release, the fish you release have a much better chance of survival when caught on a fly.

There are times, however, when the hook is more deeply taken into the throat. Although such an occurrence is rare, it does happen. In these cases, it's better to cut the fly off before you release the fish than try to remove the hook. With time, either the fish will expel this foreign object or the steel in the fly will corrode. In either case, the fish's chance of survival improves.

There may also be times when your fly is imbedded in an artery or gill arch, causing severe bleeding. Science shows that fish impaled this way have a very poor chance of surviving the next 24 hours.

When you release a fish, be sure to point and hold it in the upstream direction to let the flowing, oxygenated water pass across its gills.

If you hook a fish in an artery or gill arch and you see severe bleeding, take that fish home or back to camp—if it's legal to do so—and enjoy a nice meal.

To Take Fish or Not to Take Fish

Some anglers wonder whether they should take the fish they catch or always release them, a question that is not simple to answer. Fishing in a designated catch-and-release area neatly removes the dilemma: you must release every single fish you catch. Fishery biologists know that a certain number of fish will die from hook wounds and have taken this information into account when developing their management prescriptions for these areas.

In non-designated areas, however, the dilemma remains. Aside from what to do with a severely bleeding fish, there are other difficult questions: Should you keep a really big fish as a trophy? What if you want to try the fish to see what it tastes like? No one should feel guilty for taking a fish from waters where it's legal to do so. This doesn't mean, however, that you should stuff your creel with every fish you catch. It's true that, as a fly angler, you'll likely catch more fish—and in some cases many more—than your friends who use bait and other lures. When you're by yourself and no one else is looking, the words of Lord Baden-Powell, Lee Wulff, and other early pioneers of modern fly-fishing will hopefully come to mind: take only those fish that serve an immediate use for food, and release all others.

Temperance is in your best interest. If you and other fishers take large numbers of fish, the stock will be depleted and there will be fewer fish for you to catch next time. Lee Wulff coined the phrase, "a trout is too valuable a fish to catch but once." The same principle applies to other freshwater game fish like largemouth and smallmouth bass. Certainly it applies to select saltwater species like striped bass, bonefish, permit, tarpon, and billfish. As a fly angler, you have the responsibility of teaching others by your example. As you become increasingly proficient at enticing fish to your fly, others will look to you for advice about how to catch fish and how to best release them.

Overview of Catch-and-Release and Hooking Mortality

Various factors determine whether a released fish will survive. Considerable research funded by the Federal Aid in Sport Fish Restoration program provides some insight into what these factors are and how they may influence hooking mortality. **Hooking Location.** The location of the hook wound is thought to be the most important factor of hooking mortality. A fish hooked in the gills or throat has a much lower chance of survival than a jaw-hooked fish. Examples: In the upper Great Lakes, lake trout hooked in vital organs, like the gills or throat, experienced 71 percent mortality, compared with 7 percent for those hooked in the lower or upper jaw. In a California hatchery experiment, 56 percent of largemouth bass hooked in the throat died, while fish hooked in non-vital areas died at rates no higher than 4 percent.

Angling Method. Fish caught with artificial lures and flies generally survive better than those caught with bait. Examples: In a 3-year study in which fishers used worms and flies to catch brook trout in Michigan streams, hooking mortality ranged from 2 percent for fly-caught fish to 49 percent on fish caught with worms. A Minnesota study also found that 100 percent of the walleye caught on artificial lures survived, while 90 percent of those caught using leeches as bait survived. The hooking mortality of smallmouth bass in Michigan was at 11 percent when fishers used live minnows on a single hook versus 0 percent when fishers used artificial lures with treble hooks.

Hook Barb. There is no significant difference in the survival rate of trout and 15 marine species caught on either barbed or barbless hooks. Example: Hooking mortality rates were similar among Yellowstone cutthroat trout caught with barbed and barbless flies, barbed and barbless treble hook lures, and baited single hooks when these were not swallowed. Note: In the marine study, the number of fish landed using a barbless hook was 22 percent lower than the number of fish landed using a barbed hook. The study revealed, however, that it takes at least ten seconds longer to release a fish caught with a barbed hook.

Hook Removal. Leaving a deeply ingested hook in place usually increases the chance of survival. Examples: In Maine, landlocked Atlantic salmon that swallowed worm-baited hooks had only a 10 percent survival rate when the hook was removed, compared with a 43 percent survival rate when the hook was left in place. In New York, 59 percent of deeply hooked brown trout died when the hooks were removed, compared with 17.5 percent when they were not.

(continued on next page)

Fighting Duration. Longer playing times are thought to lead to increased mortality of released fish. Certainly, stress and muscle fatigue might make the fish more susceptible to being eaten immediately upon release. According to a Sea Grant report from Cornell University, physical exertion leads to acid buildup, and, in severe cases, blood chemistry balance is not restored and the fish may die in as many as 3 days later.

Water Temperature. Water at higher temperatures holds less oxygen and often contributes to increased mortality of released fish. Examples: The hooking mortality of lure-caught cutthroat trout in California was less than 2 percent at temperatures below 17°C (62°F), but increased by almost half when the temperature increased to 21°C (70°F). The hooking mortalities of bluegill caught in Texas with baited single hooks averaged 1 percent in winter (17°C, or 62°F) and 25 percent in summer (30°C, or 86°F).

Salinity. The effects of salinity on hooking mortality vary by species. Examples: While there is evidence that moderate salinity decreases striped bass mortality on the East Coast, the effect seems to be opposite for Coho salmon caught in an Alaskan estuary (69 percent) than among those caught upstream (12 percent) in freshwater.

Other factors to consider regarding hooking mortality include:

Hook Design. Circle hooks that typically impale the outer mouthparts versus traditional hooks that may lodge indiscriminately in the mouth or deeper into the gut.

Hook Size. Larger hooks may cause mouthpart damage, but are unlikely to be taken deeply into the throat.

Number of Hooks. Because of their bulk, treble hooks are less likely to reach vital organs.

Catch Handling. Getting fish back into the water quickly helps ensure a greater chance of survival.

Release Techniques. Keeping the fish pointed upstream until it swims away on its own improves its chances of survival.

Fish Size. Larger fish generally need a longer recovery period.

Sources

Lucy, J. A., A. L. Studholme, editors. 2002. Catch and release in marine recreational fisheries. American Fisheries Society, Symposium 30, Bethesda, Maryland.

Malchoff, M. H., M. P. Voiland and D. B. MacNeill. 1992. Guidelines to increase survival of released sport fish. Cornell Cooperative Extension Fact Sheet.

Muoneke, M. I. and W. M. Childress. 1994. Hooking mortality: a review for recreational fisheries. *Reviews in Fisheries Science*. 2(2): 123–155.

Schaeffer, J.S. and E.M. Hoffman. 2002. Performance of barbed and barbless hooks in a marine recreational fishery. *North American Journal of Fishery Management*. 22: 229–235.

Exceptions to Catch-and-Release Practice

As I suggested earlier, there are exceptions that allow us to take some fish home to eat, as long as we don't take more fish than we absolutely need. In Alaska, for example, there are five species of Pacific salmon that annually return to their natal rivers to spawn. For the most part, these anadromous fish populations are healthy and are quite heavily managed. After they spawn, the fish die, leaving the nutrients from their decaying bodies for the next generation of fish. Managers have estimated the numbers of returning fish that are needed to sustain the fishery. Once this escapement quota is reached, pretty much all the remaining fish just returning from the sea can be harvested without any impact on the future fishery. Clearly the biologists have taken into account the available spawning habitat, and what they don't want is one fish destroying the redd (nest) of another. In other words, too many fish in the spawning areas can be as big a problem as too few. To address this side of the issue, the managers may actually increase the daily creel limit to encourage anglers to take more fish.

TIP: Daily creel limits are designated by each state, and they may vary daily or among lakes, ponds, and even among rivers. Check the current regulations for your fishing destination before you leave to be sure that you have the most up-to-date information.

Another argument for taking more fish is offered by native Alaskans, who feel that to catch and release some of these salmon would be a sacrilege to a gift offered by Mother Ocean. They believe that returning salmon are part of a religious ritual, and the natives' part of that ritual is to harvest fish as a way of sustaining their culture. Surely, this philosophy also has to be acknowledged and respected.

Still another consideration is the survival rate of stocked fish once the cool waters of springtime begin to heat up in the summer. Massachusetts and other state fishery managers stock many small lakes and ponds with trout in the early spring. The intention of this practice is to provide recreational angling in the months prior to summer, when the ponds will warm up and no longer be able to sustain a trout fishery. This makes for good fishing in the spring, but what happens to these trout in the summer? If they can't find a spring outlet or a cold-water stream, they likely will head to the pond's colder bottom waters. Unfortunately these trout will be caught in a no-win situation as summer progresses. They can't return to the surface because the water is too warm; warmer water doesn't hold as much oxygen as colder water. Unfortunately, the bottom will provide only temporary sanctuary. Accumulated organic matter at the bottom of lakes and ponds will deplete oxygen levels as it decomposes. Trout that aren't brought home for dinner might suffocate anyway.

Other Ways to Limit Fishing Mortality

An easy strategy you can use to further minimize fishing mortality is to match your fishing tackle to the type of fish you're trying to catch. Don't, for example, use a 3-weight rod to catch a 5-pound fish. Can it be done? Sure, but be advised that the longer the fight, the more exhausted the fish will be and the longer it will take to recover. As an angler, you have the responsibility of staying with that fish until it can swim away on its own power.

Some fish have a swim bladder—an organ that helps fish maintain neutral buoyancy. When one of these fish is pulled from the depths too quickly, gases in the bladder expand. If the gases aren't vented, the bladder inflates like a balloon and may extend out the fish's mouth. A fish released in this condition may be unable to dive downward. Instead it will remain on the water's surface, making it vulnerable to predators. To resolve this problem, carefully puncture the inflated swim bladder and then release the fish by plunging it head first into the water to help get it started toward deeper water. The bladder may heal, sometimes in as little as four days.

One myth to dispel here is the belief that any fish that swims away will survive another day. The severely bleeding fish we discussed earlier is a prime example of one that will not. Also, all fish need oxygen to survive, and some fish—including trout—need higher oxygen levels than others. Again, when water's temperature increases, its ability to hold oxygen decreases. A tired fish will recover faster in colder water than in warm water. In addition, while it's recovering, it may still be vulnerable to predators, especially immediately upon release.

TIP: In warmer months, it's wise—and better for the fish—to shift from fishing for trout to fishing for warm-water species such as bass, bluegill, crappie, or saltwater fish.

Some years ago, while fishing the out-flow of a river in Maine, I caught a nice 14-inch landlocked Atlantic salmon. By Atlantic salmon standards this was not a big fish, but on a 5-weight rod it was quite spectacular. After it made several wonderful leaps, I was able to bring the fish to the side of my canoe. Just before I released it, I noticed a very big bass holding in about 1 foot of water below where I was about to drop the salmon. The bass was watching that salmon much like a well-trained dog standing on its hind legs waits for a treat. Had I released the salmon as I normally would have, there would have been one less land-locked Atlantic salmon in that lake. Instead, I brought the salmon to the other side of the canoe. The bass quickly disappeared, and after a moment I dropped the salmon into the water. I hope it at least had half a chance to get away.

Another time I was fishing for bonefish in the Bahamas. When I was about to release a fish, I noticed a lingering black-tipped shark just waiting to have a bonefish dinner. I chased the shark away by nudging it with my rod tip, and then I successfully released the bonefish.

If you notice that larger predators are becoming habituated to your fishing location in order to get an easy meal, perhaps it's time to move elsewhere.

Hook Styles and Their Impact on Hooking Mortality

Fish hooks of one form or another have been around for thousands of years. Prehistoric Alaskans, for example, were even known to have circle hooks carved from bone or ivory. Today, hook manufacturers from Europe, America and Japan offer every imaginable hook style, size and shape an angler might need. Many are chemically sharpened, which means an acid dip has been applied to the hooks to create a straight and sharp point that will quickly penetrate the most dense jaw tissue of a fish. Just back from the hook point, there is a tag of metal cut into the wire called the *barb*. The barb is designed to prevent the hook from easily backing out once the fish is impaled.

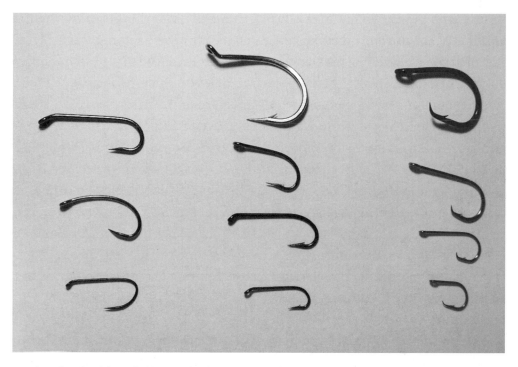

Hook styles: barbless (left), standard (center), and circle (right).

There is no significant scientific evidence, however, to indicate that barbless hooks actually decrease hooking mortality. In a review paper, researchers at Texas A&M University determined that most hooking mortality is a result of where in the body a fish is hooked, how deeply the hook penetrates the fish's throat, whether the fish is bleeding severely, and the level of the fish's exhaustion upon release. Hook style didn't really enter the equation to a large degree, although barbless hooks can help you release fish more quickly. In general, it's best to check the laws in the states where you will be fishing, as some states may mandate the use of barbless hooks in specific waters. Several states have withdrawn their barbless hook regulations, while others may still require them in certain areas or at certain times.

There has been a trend toward circle-shaped hooks in recent years, especially in specific saltwater fisheries where catch-and-release is a prominent management strategy. Because of their shape, these hooks generally catch fish in the outer mouthparts. Hooking mortality that results from deeply penetrating hooks, hook swallowing, or the piercing of vital blood vessels is almost nonexistent with circle hooks.

A couple of summers ago, I wanted to determine whether small circle hooks, specifically size 14, held any advantage over traditional hook shapes. For this unofficial experiment, I tied my Black Gnat Parachute pattern on some Eagle Claw circle hooks. In Alaska, Arctic grayling abound. I compared the success of identical patterns tied on the different hook styles, switching back and forth between them.

Here is what I found. First, size 14 circle hooks are more difficult to extract from a fish's mouth than traditional hooks. Second, as expected, circle hooks caught fish in the outer mouthparts. Third, circle hooks can catch more fish if the angler is inattentive and uses poor line control techniques.

While the latter discovery might initially appear to be an advantage to a new angler, I am reluctant to endorse circle hooks for this purpose. Such use could become a crutch, allowing the angler to become lazy. To be a competent angler, you *must* practice good line control techniques. When I used traditional hooks for my Black Gnat Parachute and I exercised good line control, I was able to approximately double the number of fish I caught in the same time period. The point is that there is no substitute for good line control if you want to catch fish.

Another disadvantage of the small circle hooks is that they're not widely available. If you're not a flytier, the patterns you readily need might not be available for purchase.

HUR 15

CARE AND MAINTENANCE
OF EQUIPMENT

In general, your fly equipment can be a bit more costly than traditional fishing gear. Since fly equipment represents an investment in time and dollars, the better care you give it, the longer it will last and the more value you'll get from it. In every instance, I simply recommend you follow the manufacturers' care recommendations. In the absence of such guidance, you may just have to use your own good judgment. Here are some simple principles that universally apply.

Sunlight, heat, and chemicals will destroy your fly line.

The plastics in fly lines are vulnerable to sunlight, insect repellent, and other chemicals that might be around you. For example, don't put 100 percent DEET insect repellent on your hands and then cast a few moments later. The same advice applies if you use aerosol spray insect repellent. Instead, try the stick insect repellent by Cutter, which is similar to a small deodorant roll-on.

I have a friend who uses Armor All to clean his fly lines, but I'm reluctant to clean mine with anything other than a mild soap-and-water solution or one of the cleaning products sold specifically for cleaning and recoating fly lines. At the very least, rinse your equipment with clean fresh water after each use.

Try to keep your fly lines from baking in the hot sun. If you store your fishing gear in your parked vehicle (like most of us), try to park in the shade, or at least crack the windows a bit to let out the heat. A hot car goes a long way toward killing your $60 fly lines.

Rotate your inventory of tippet and tapered leaders.

Over time, all of your expensive tapered leaders and tippet material can deteriorate. If you store these items in a cool, dry area away from sunlight, you can extend their useful life. With an indelible pen, write the date of purchase on the packaging, and plan to use the older items first. Then place the items in a sealed plastic storage bag and store it in a convenient place where you'll know where to find it later.

Putting your stuff away wet invites disaster.

Mildew, mold, rust, and other nasty things can result if you put your gear away wet. The best strategy is to ensure that all your fishing equipment is dry before you store it. Mesh laundry bags, which provide ventilation, are excellent containers for bulky items like wading shoes and chest waders. Keeping these items out of direct sunlight can also greatly improve longevity.

Salt water corrodes.

Any time two different metals come in contact with one another in salt water, a mini battery is formed and one of those metals will corrode. You may have heard of galvanic action, and this is a prime example. Be sure to thoroughly rinse all reel and other metal parts—including metal reel seats—with fresh water. Allow the wet parts to air-dry somewhere out of direct sunlight.

Don't put your fly rod on the roof of your vehicle.

I admit that sometimes I'm a very forgetful person. More than once I have put my fly rod on top of my vehicle while I take off my waders and stow my other gear. Sure enough, a few miles down the road I remember the rod. Upon backtracking I might find a) the rod intact; b) the rod broken; or c) nothing, because someone else has already picked it up. To avoid such a mistake, lean your rod against the driver's side mirror. Since adopting this new practice, I have yet to drive off and leave a rod on the side of the road.

Sand, mud, and coral chips make terrible lubricants.

It's a fact of nature that, somehow, the most abrasive grit seeks out and finds the most delicate parts of your reel. Bearings, drags, and adjustment knobs have all been known to malfunction because of the accumulation of foreign particulates. If your reel takes an accidental mud bath or gets placed on a beach, take off the spool and rinse it as best you can with clean, fresh water.

Dried fish slime stinks.

I have a small landing net made by Gudebrod that folds very nicely onto my chest pack belt. Since I catch a lot of fish, it's always exposed to a fresh dose of fish slime. If I don't take time to rinse it off between catches, it gets a buildup of slime. After a day or two in my vehicle, the net begins to smell like rotting fish. Now, while I might not think it's that bad, my wife never fails to remind me why she doesn't like to ride in my vehicle.

Fly rods are not designed to be stepped on.

Some years ago my son went on a scouting trip to Maine. After fishing one evening, he put his rod in the back of a scout leader's vehicle. Unbeknownst to him, while rummaging around for something in the same vehicle, another scout accidentally stepped on and broke the rod. It certainly wasn't the end of the world, but it did abruptly end my son's ability to fish on that trip. The message here is put your gear away properly after each use.

Most rods come in a hard, protective tube. Manufacturers provide these tubes for an obvious reason: to protect your rod when you're not using it. As an alternative, you can suspend a rod rack from the inside roof of your vehicle. Mine holds three rods and provides quick access and relatively safe storage after each day of fishing. Since most people don't walk on the inside roof of an SUV, I figure I have more than an even chance of keeping my rods intact.

Broken hooks don't catch fish, and rusty hooks are not sharp.

Sometimes a hook will snap just at the bend, leaving the fly intact. If you're just looking at the tied part of the hook, all looks fine. The first clue that you have a problem is when you continue to get strikes but never seem to hook a fish. After a number of misses, check the fly. Sometimes the hook part is entirely gone, or perhaps it has somehow been straightened. Neither situation is effective if you really like to catch fish! As a rule you should check your flies up close every once in a while, whether you're hooking fish or not, just to be sure things are as they should be.

Rusty hooks can also be a problem. Rust often develops when you put your flies away wet. A wet fly invites rust, and rusty hooks are not as sharp as new hooks, nor are they as strong. Once again Murphy's Law will rule: if you catch the largest fish on a rusty hook, the hook will break and you lose a lifetime trophy.

Never put a damp fly in your fly box. Allow it to air-dry, and then put it away. If your flies get wet because you fished in the rain or fell in, be sure to take each fly out of your fly box and let it dry thoroughly before putting it back. Remember, keeping hooks—and, for that matter, all your fishing gear—in serviceable condition is a way of protecting your investment.

Missing or broken rod tips decrease your casting distance.

Rod tips are the thinnest part of the rod and are therefore easy to break. Rod manufacturers design their rods to cast effectively. Decreasing the rod length even by an inch or two really upsets the design specification that the rod company worked so hard to achieve. Be especially careful not to whack the rod tip into the ground, around a tree branch, or some other hard or immovable object.

Leaky boots are very uncomfortable.

Most fly anglers wear boots or hip or chest waders because they really like to keep their legs warm and feet dry. With time, wear and tear will degrade a boot's ability to keep the water on the outside. Plodding through briars, over barbed wire fences, or over other sharp objects will—with certainty—increase the permeability of your waterproof boots. Sunlight is known to degrade the ability of boot fabric to repel water. Most boot manufacturers do supply a small patch kit that can repair small punctures or rips. The objective here, however, is to avoid getting any small punctures or rips in your boots so you can save the patch kit for your bicycle tires.

Sunburn hurts.

Now, I know your skin isn't considered part of your fishing equipment, but I can assure you that if you have a bad case of sunburn, you won't want to go fishing. Take reasonable precaution by wearing quality clothing and a wide-brim hat, and use a high-SPF sunscreen.

If you can't find it, you don't have it.

Many anglers use fishing vests that have twenty or more pockets, some of which may be on the inside lining. With all of these places to store stuff, only the most organized folks can actually remember where everything is or should be. Having an organizational plan isn't such a bad idea when you pocket fishing items like tippet, leaders, nippers, floatant, thermometer, fly boxes, insect repellent, sunscreen, sunglasses, knot tying tools, and whatever else you wish to carry in your vest. If there is rhyme and reason to the placement of items, you'll be able to find them quickly and easily. Always be sure to put things back in the same place. Time spent fishing is precious, and you don't want to waste an inordinate amount of it looking for this or that.

Wash new clothing before you wear it.

If you're planning a fishing trip and intend to bring along any new gear or clothing, be sure to give it a trial run before you go. If you wait until you're far from home to try these things out for the first time, you may find yourself in an unpleasant predicament.

Once when I went fishing in a foreign country, I brought along a brand new pair of fleece pants that I'd bought just before I left, to wear inside my chest waders. I had neither worn them nor washed them before the trip. On the last day or two of the trip, I gave them a try, and, whether it was because of the dye or the fabric, my legs broke out in the most poison-ivy-like rash you have ever seen. Fortunately I wore socks and underwear, so my feet and groin were spared, and I had some hydrocortisone ointment that helped until I was able to see my doctor back home. If I'd checked the pants out before I left home, or had I simply washed them, I could have been spared this unpleasant experience.

Small cuts, abrasions, and knots reduce line strength.

Any time your tapered leader or tippet scrapes against a rock, tree, or stream bottom, or rubs across a fish's teeth, you're creating small nicks on the line. Over time, these nicks will reduce your line strength. Check your leader or tippet by feeling it every once in a while as you're fishing, and if you feel cuts, abrasions, or knots, cut these sections out and replace them with new material. Don't be lazy and think it will be OK, because it won't.

When you do replace damaged leader or tippet, remember to put the old stuff in one of those twenty or so pockets in your fishing vest. Try the pocket where you put your candy wrappers and other trash that will accumulate during the day. At the end of each fishing day, properly dispose of the trash.

Torn nets don't hold fish.

I have seen this happen more than once: a small tear in a landing net allows a fish to go in one side of the net bag and out the other. Once that fish's head or tail finds the hole, its continuous movement enlarges the hole and, oops, off it goes. Repair holes as they occur. At times you may have to replace the whole net. When you do, I encourage you to consider a soft, fine mesh replacement net that's fish friendly.

HOUR 16

LICENSES, FLY-FISHING ETIQUETTE, AND LEAVE-NO-TRACE PRACTICES

Like any sport, fly-fishing has its share of rules and recommended modes of good behavior with which every fisher should become familiar and then follow. A good angler will always play by the rules, adhere to safety principles, respect property, and be courteous to others. After all, when we play clean and fair, everyone has a lot more fun, and we may even have some great stories to tell at the end of the day.

Fishing Licenses

First and foremost, make sure your fishing license is current before you head to your favorite fishing hole. No question about it, fishing without a license will get you in trouble every time. Also make sure you have all the necessary stamps (e.g., land stamps, trout stamps, saltwater stamps, etc.) affixed to your license if they're required by the state in which you'll be fishing. If the state requires you to sign the stamp, do so in ballpoint ink, as other types of ink may run if they become wet.

States use license fees to help match annual federal Sport Fish Restoration allocations, and the combined revenues are invested to improve your fishing experience. The cost of a license is generally low: you can fish all season for less than the price of a dinner, a movie, gas, and a babysitter.

Many states conveniently sell licenses online. You can contact most state fish and wildlife agencies by going to www.IAFWA.org/members/state-agency-websites.htm. The problem with an online purchase, however, is you're unable to speak with anyone regarding local requirements or other legal mandates associated with your desired fishing destination. For that additional information, you'll have to contact your local district biologist, fishery manager or conservation officer.

TIP: Just about every state has at least one free fishing day a year during National Fishing and Boating Week (usually in early June). Contact each state's fish and wildlife agency to find out the specific days.

General Fly-Fishing Etiquette

I have fished on opening day of trout season and participated in combat fishing on the Russian River in Alaska, where fishers are spaced about 6 feet apart. This is tight fishing, and, as long as everyone is catching fish or otherwise having fun, it works. Sometimes it's as much a social event as it is a fishing opportunity. If everyone cooperates, even this kind of fishing can be enjoyable.

There are no laws saying how you should behave when fly-fishing. Rather, the Golden Rule applies: do unto other anglers as you would have them do unto you. Clearly, it just comes down to respect. If you see someone fishing, don't walk into the river right on top of that angler. Rather, go several hundred yards upstream or downstream before plodding into the river. Give the other angler as much space as possible. If you must cross at a given spot, ask permission. If someone arrived at the pool before you, respect his or her turn, and if you must fish there, come back later or wait until the other person moves on. In smaller rivers, anglers fishing upstream have the right-of-way, so the angler fishing downstream should get out of the river and re-enter and resume fishing well downstream of the person fishing upstream.

Unwritten Rules of Etiquette

1. Respect your fellow anglers.
2. Ask permission before passing through a fellow angler's space.
3. When sharing a pool, wait your turn.
4. Anglers fishing upstream have the right-of-way.
5. Be mindful of your own noise.
6. Don't converse with a focused angler unless invited to do so.
7. Respect property and ask permission of private land owners to cross their land.

I have had curious canoeists and kayakers approach me to ask how I'm doing. Sometimes as they make their way over, they drift over the very spot I'm fishing. I know these are well-meaning folks, but their curiosity sometimes destroys my opportunity to catch a particular fish. Had they known to ask, I would have suggested they go quietly behind me, and everyone would have been happy.

Fish can hear noise, and skittish fish become even more wary when they hear unfamiliar sounds. Fish can also feel the vibrations you create when you stomp along the stream bank, so walk softly. In general, don't be loud.

When I'm really working a fish, I'm concentrating very intently. If you come up and start a conversation, you might not encounter my most pleasant disposition. Other anglers are the same way, and it may not be the best idea to strike up a lengthy conversation at that moment. If you must, merely say hello. A hello will either initiate more conversation or not. It's the angler's call. If he or she simply says hello, offers a polite wave, or merely smiles, take the hint and quietly move along.

Leave-No-Trace Practices

Leave-No-Trace is a program designed to help you practice good stewardship of our natural resources. By following the principles below and caring for these special places, you'll more fully enjoy nature. And you'll ensure that, after you have returned home, others will enjoy these places, too.

Know before you go.

As they say in the scouts, be prepared! Don't forget clothes that will protect you from the cold, heat, rain, ice, or snow. Use maps and a compass to guide you so you won't get lost. Don't rely entirely on GPS (carry extra batteries). Learn about the areas you'll visit. Read books, search the Web, and talk to knowledgeable people before you go. The more you know about these places, the more fun you'll have and the more you'll appreciate what you see.

Choose the right path.

Stay on the main trail, and don't wander off by yourself. Steer clear of flowers and small trees. Some habitats, like tundra, are especially delicate and, once damaged, may not recover for many years. Use existing campsites, or camp at least one hundred paces from roads, trails, and water.

Trash your trash.

Pack it in and pack it out. Put litter and food scraps in appropriate trash receptacles or carry them out. Use outhouses when available. If they're not and you have to "go," act like a cat; bury your feces in a small hole 4 to 8 inches deep and at least one hundred paces from water. Similarly, keep water clean; do not pour wash water into lakes, ponds, rivers, or streams. Collecting and properly disposing any litter or trash you find is also a good practice. If you don't pick it up, who will?

Leave what you find.

Leave plants, rocks, and historical items as you find them so the next person can enjoy them, too. Treat these items with respect. If you think you have found something extraordinary, report your find to an appropriate authority. While they may already know about it, a special site previously unknown may need additional protection.

Possession of migratory bird feathers, especially those from eagles, requires a federal permit and could result in stiff penalties if you don't have one. If you find such feathers, leave them.

Good campsites are found, not made. Don't make permanent changes to the campsite. When you leave, it should look very much like it did when you found it.

TIP: When you purchase your fishing license, be sure to ask for a copy of the latest fishing regulations for the area you'll be fishing. Here you might also find information or references to camping, use of fire and any restrictions on disturbing wildlife. The state's fish and wildlife division's website is also a good first source of these kinds of information.

Use fire with caution.

Use a camp stove for cooking. Stoves make it easier to cook and clean up. If you want to build a small campfire, be sure to follow all guidelines, regulations, and permits. Use existing fire rings. Control all fires, and use only dead wood you find on the beach or ground. Burn all wood to ash, and be sure that the fire is completely out and cold before you go to sleep or vacate the campsite. Remove and carry out any unburned trash buried in the ash. As a nice gesture, leave some extra firewood stacked neatly for the next party.

Respect wildlife.

Wild animals can kill you. Observe wild animals from a distance; never approach, feed, or follow them. When in the vicinity of large animals like moose, bear, buffalo, or elk, don't risk your life positioning for the picture of a lifetime. Leave it up to the photographers from *National Geographic* to take the close-up photos. Large wild animals are unpredictable.

Feeding wild animals a human diet is unhealthy, and it may encourage a bad habit. Protect your food by appropriately storing meals and trash.

Leave Rover at home.

Keep pets under control at all times or leave them at home. I don't recommend fishing with them at all. Recently, a few friends and I went fishing for bonefish on a shallow tidal flat, and a nice golden retriever followed us out. Just as I spotted a tailing fish—a fish that was bottom feeding with its tail out of the water—so did the dog. As I was making my first cast, the dog charged full speed at the fish, frightening it into the next sea. I had a few choice words for that poor dog!

Be kind to other visitors.

Make sure the fun you have in the outdoors doesn't bother anyone else. Remember that other visitors are there to enjoy the outdoor experience as well. Listen to nature, and avoid making loud noises.

If you see a fellow angler who needs something, offer to help. Remember, everyone is out there for enjoyment, and sometimes it's the little things you can do that will make a big difference in another angler's day. You never know if, in return, that angler will offer you a fly, a most valuable tip, or even the location of a secret fishing hole. At the very least you'll gain a friend, and in this world we need as many friends as we can get!

Time Check

Well, I'm sure we managed to gain some time over the last few hours and that your progress toward becoming a competent fly angler hasn't suffered for it. In the next few hours, we will learn additional casting techniques, how to fish with a guide and from a boat, and—perhaps most important of all—how to fish safely.

HUR 17

ADVANCED CASTING
TECHNIQUES

Now that you know how to cast thirty feet, I'm anticipating that you'll want to learn how to cast farther. In this chapter we'll look at some techniques to improve distance, plus I'll teach you how to properly shoot fly line.

Once you've learned to cast thirty feet of fly line, it's relatively easy to cast forty feet, fifty feet, and even sixty feet. With today's excellent weight-forward lines and the design of modern graphite rods, these distances are achievable if you continue to practice and perfect your technique.

Building Line Speed

On weight-forward fly lines, most of the line's weight is located in the first thirty or forty feet of line. It is the mass of this front section that bends and loads the rod when you begin to cast. The rest of the line is running line. Your goal is to build line speed using the first thirty feet.

1. Measure thirty feet of fly line from where the leader is attached. With an indelible marker, make a bold, readily distinguishable mark about ½-inch-long or so, at thirty feet. This mark will indicate where the heaviest section of the weight-forward line ends.

2. Start with the thirty-foot mark at the rod tip, and practice making thirty-foot casts. Let the fly line fall to the ground in front of you when you complete a cast, then start over. Once you can do this with confidence, begin false casting (see "A Closer Look at the False Cast" below). Again, pinch the fly line to the rod grip with the middle finger of your casting hand. Don't get fancy with your noncasting hand just yet; perhaps the best place for it right now is in your pocket.

As you false cast you should begin to feel the line speed increase as energy is transferred from the rod to the line.

A Closer Look at the False Cast

Essentially, a false cast is one in which you let the line unfurl behind you, then bring it forward and allow it to unfurl in front, and then repeat the rearward sequence. The line never touches the water; hence the name of the cast.

Begin your cast and snap-stop the rod at the 1 o'clock stopping position. Then snap-stop it at the 10 o'clock stopping position. Repeat.

In fishing situations you will false cast whenever your fly has completed its downstream drift and it needs to be picked up and cast back upstream for another presentation. False casting is also used to air dry your fly if it begins to sink.

Shooting Line

Once you understand false casting and feel confident with your technique, you're ready to shoot line and, with increasing practice, double your casting distances. Just follow these steps.

1. Align your thirty-foot fly line mark with the rod tip. From the reel, strip about ten feet of running line. Let it fall on the ground just in front of you.

2. Again, take a moment to stretch the first thirty feet of fly line as you did in Hours 8–9.

3. With the thumb and index finger of your noncasting hand, pinch the fly line about a foot below the first stripping guide (the guide just above the reel). The ten feet of the running line should still be lying on the ground in front of you. Check again to make sure the thirty-foot mark is at the rod tip and the noncasting hand is firmly holding the fly line just below the first stripping guide. When you begin your casting sequence, the noncasting hand will remain stationary.

4. Begin your false casting sequence to increase line speed. During this part of the cast, maintain the pinch on the fly line with your noncasting hand.

5. After two or three false casts, stop the rod tip at the 10 o'clock position and release your grasp on the fly line in your noncasting hand. The added line speed you created while false casting will carry the additional ten feet forward over the water.

6. As you release the fly line, use the thumb and index finger of your noncasting hand to form an "OK" sign around the line. The additional running line will travel through the O formed by your fingers—and will help reduce the possibility of a memory coil jamming in the stripping guide and ruining your cast.

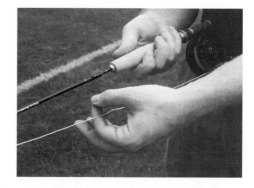

7. Practice this 10 o'clock release several more times until you learn the precise moment at which to release your fly line.

The OK sign helps the fly line smoothly travel into the rod when you are shooting line.

Once you have mastered shooting an additional ten feet of line, repeat the process by adding line in 5- or 10-foot increments. Always go back to your mark at thirty feet to begin your lifting and false casting. As you continue practicing, you'll learn that as line speed increases, so does your casting distance, as does your casting accuracy. Eventually you will be able to cast to fifty or even sixty feet. And this brings us to the next casting technique.

Hauling

A technique called *hauling* will help you to cast even farther than simply shooting line. Hauling is when your noncasting hand pulls the line downward as you cast, which adds even more speed and distance.

1. Follow steps 1 through 4 of "Shooting Line" (above). This time, however, your noncasting hand will do a bit more work and contribute to the forward and rearward line speed.

2. Lift the first thirty feet of fly line off the water and initiate your rearward cast. Raise your rod tip and, at the same time, pull the line you're pinching with your noncasting hand rapidly downward about 6 to 10 inches or so. Start the pull when the rod tip is at 9 o'clock, and finish it when you abruptly stop the rod tip at 1 o'clock. The thirty feet of line should fly out and unfurl behind you more quickly than when you shoot line. This is known as the first haul, or single haul. After you complete the first haul, you should allow your line-pinching hand to drift upward toward your rod holding hand. This subtle movement will position it better for making the second haul on your forecast.

3. When the fly line has fully unfurled behind you, apply thumb pressure for the forward cast and start the second haul by pulling downward again on the line with your noncasting hand.

4. Snap-stop the rod at the 10 o'clock position to allow the forward part of the loop to form. At the same moment release the fly line in

When preparing to do a single haul, grasp the fly line with your non-casting hand about one foot below the first stripping guide. To get the most energy out of your lift, keep the rod tip pointed low and toward the water.

As you raise the rod tip to lift the line off the water's surface, draw the fly line sharply downward. This motion will add line speed to your rearward stroke.

your noncasting hand. Then follow the rod tip through by gradually lowering the rod to a more horizontal position that points at your target. The thirty plus feet of additional line length will then sail out over the water.

TIP: Throughout the hauling sequence, maintain the same pinch point on the line. Hauling any more than the recommended 6 to 10 inches will foul up the timing, and when that happens your casting distance will suffer.

A Closer Look at the Physics of Hauling

No Haul

Haul

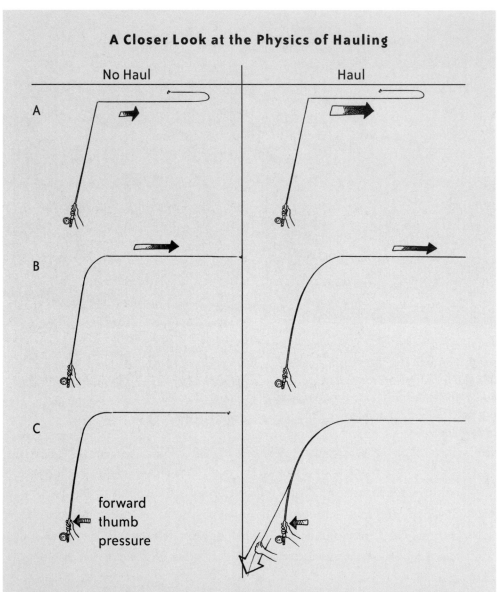

Notice the differences in line speed and rod loading between a cast having no haul vs. a single haul (A); the load transferred to the rod by the fly line when it's fully unfurled vs. the greater load caused by the fly line moving rearward and fully unfurling faster as a result of the single haul (B); the extra load added to the rod by the forward thumb pressure vs. the additive load of the second haul combined with the forward thumb pressure (C).

If you recall from our discussion about the mechanics of fly casting from Hours 8–9 (page 64), it is during the loading process that energy is transferred from the fly line to the rod. The purpose of a haul is to add even more load to the rod, which will add line speed and distance to your cast. You will notice that the rod bends deeper when you execute a haul; this is due to the added load.

During the rearward haul, or *first haul*, the combined motion of lifting the rod tip and pulling downward on the line loads the rod and increases line speed as the fly line moves from the water to the air. When you snap-stop the rod tip at the 1 o'clock position the energy transfers back to the fly line as it moves rearward. The same thing holds true for the forward haul, or *second haul*. The combined motion of moving the rod forward and the downward pull on the line adds even more load to the rod.

When you snap-stop at the 10 o'clock position the cumulative energy of both hauls is transferred from the rod to the fly line. Just release the fly line in your non-casting hand and the running line will sail off.

Other Casting Techniques

There are some additional techniques that will help you cast even farther, but, as I said earlier, I'm not convinced a longer cast will catch more fish.

Line Release

Up until this point, we actually were casting only the first 30 feet of fly line, but once you get the technique figured out, you can add a few more feet of fly line to your cast by shooting a few feet on your forecast and backcast. Here's how.

During the backcast, let a few feet of line slip between the fingers of your noncasting hand. This extra line will add a little weight to the fly line being cast. Then, during the forward part of the false cast, release a little more line. As you do this, your arm will have to work a little harder to keep the extra line in the air, but the added energy and line speed—when released during the presentation cast—will add distance.

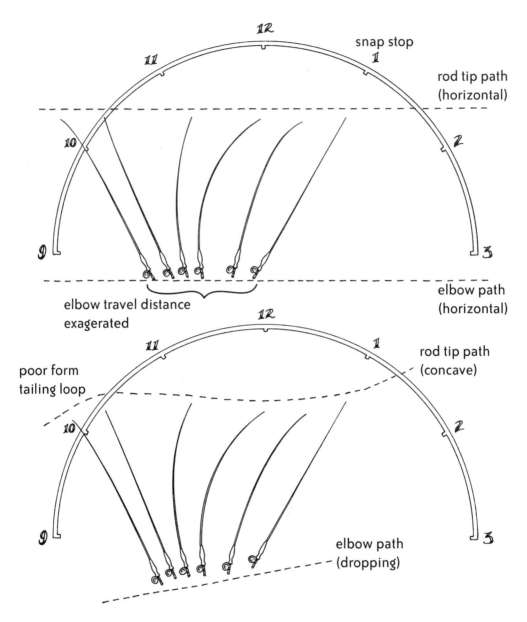

The movement of your elbow is what adds the extra energy to the cast. Always keep your elbow on a horizontal plane. This way the casting loop will successfully unfurl and the fly will stay above the rod tip and above the front section of the fly line. If you drop your elbow below the horizontal plane, the terminal end of the fly line will drop below the front section of the line and cause a tailing loop.

Rearward Arm Shift

The rearward arm shift is a very simple technique that will add distance to your cast, but it must be done properly or you'll end up with a tailing loop. The secret is to keep your elbow on the same horizontal plane throughout the cast. After you snap-stop the rod tip at the 1 o'clock position, and while the fly line is unfurling out behind you, let your casting arm pivot at the shoulder and float backward about a foot. Then, when you begin moving the rod tip forward, bring your elbow forward about a foot and a half. Do not raise or drop your elbow during this rearward and forward movement; your elbow must remain on the same horizontal plane throughout the cast.

When the rod tip reaches the 10 o'clock position, release the line from your noncasting hand. Let the rod follow through until it's parallel to the water's surface and the tip is pointed just above your target area.

The Water Haul

The water haul is another casting technique that adds line speed to the cast.

1. Start with thirty feet of fly line on the water and ten feet of additional line stripped off the reel. Pinch the fly line with your noncasting hand.
2. Raise the rod tip swiftly from the water as you initiate your backcast. Feel the added resistance as the line is drawn up into the air. This resistance helps add more energy, or load, to the rod.
3. As you complete the backcast, release a few extra feet of fly line. Then continue the casting sequence forward, letting the fly line fall to the water.
4. Immediately lift the line once again to initiate another backcast. If you do this with precise timing, the extra tension of the line coming off the water will add more energy to the rod, and the combined energy will be released during the presentation cast.

The water haul can add distance to your cast, but it also has the disadvantage of slapping, sloshing, or otherwise disturbing the water as you aggressively lay down then lift the line. The added noise and disturbance of the water haul will surely spook some fish, so only use it with discretion. Again, although it's useful to learn these advanced casting techniques, in most situations you probably won't need to cast more than thirty feet to catch fish.

HUR 18

FISHING WITH A GUIDE AND FISHING FROM A SMALL BOAT

Fishing with a Guide

The fastest way to learn where to fish and what flies to use is to hire a fishing guide. Although you may pay $200 or more a day for a guide, it's the way to go if your goal is to catch fish in a limited amount of time. If a guide has been in business a while, he should have a thorough knowledge of the area in which you'll be fishing and should be able to put you right on top of the fish. And although a guide can't guarantee fish, he or she should be able to increase your chances of success. All guides want to see their clients happy, so they will do everything possible to help you catch fish.

How to Find a Guide

In order to find a good guide, you need to do some research. See if any of your fishing friends or local tackle shop can recommend one, or search online for guides in the area in which you're planning to fish. When you have the names of some guides, find out what credentials they have.

Are they certified? Be sure to ask any guide you contact for references, and then follow up by e-mail or telephone.

If you have preferences like nonsmoking or special dietary needs, let the guide know before you go on a trip together. Also, prior to going out with the guide, ask what is expected of you and what you can expect. Will lunch, drinks, flies, and gear be provided? If so, do these items cost extra or are they part of the package? Find out what the refund policy is if the weather is bad or if you or the guide can't make the trip for some reason. Does the guide encourage tips and, if so, at what percentage? Remember, guiding is a livelihood; these folks rely on your fees as their income. If the guide does something extra-special for you, be sure to express your appreciation accordingly.

Once you arrange where and when you'll meet the guide, make sure you're on time! You want to get what you're paying for. Most guides today have cell phones; be sure to call if you're delayed.

The Client and Guide Relationship

Guides, like all people, have varying personalities. Some are quiet while others like to pass the time telling jokes or fishing stories. Just think of them as part of the entire fishing experience. The common thread among the guides I've been with is they want you to catch fish. Since I like to fish, I fish hard. I'm always trying to make that extra cast or cast into that difficult spot. Guides generally appreciate an angler who works hard to catch fish. When a guide sees his clients working hard, he may work harder to put them in the best spots.

Communication is the key to a successful day. Most guides will pick up on your casting abilities fairly quickly and will make adjustments. For instance, he might suggest a better casting angle or move you to a spot where the sun or wind will be more helpful to your presentation. If, however, you're having trouble casting in a specific direction, don't be reluctant to ask the guide if another angle might be possible. If something is bothering you, find a nice way to mention the issue and ask the guide if the problem can be resolved. Since everyone is there to catch fish and have a good time, it pays to speak up if something feels amiss.

The guide should also provide standards of acceptable behavior. In general, excessive drinking is wrong and dangerous while fishing. No one likes loud, boorish behavior, and on a small boat or in a fishing camp it can be particularly hard to take.

Treat your guide as a friend. When the guide makes a suggestion, a wise angler will usually consider it, and many will adopt it. Clearly, the guide is the expert on the waters you're fishing, and you'll do well to heed any advice he or she offers.

Fishing from a Small Vessel

Fishing from a small boat, canoe, kayak, or float tube can be a lot of fun. Each of these vessels will help you reach fish that are otherwise inaccessible from shore. Before you embark, however, make sure you take the necessary safety precautions.

PFDs and Other Necessities

First and foremost on your safety list should be serviceable personal floatation devices (PFDs). Some states require that you wear a PFD in certain kinds of boats, like canoes and kayaks, so be sure to check the laws and regulations of any state in which you plan to boat and fish. Again, your local tackle shop can usually provide this information. If laws permit you to stow your PFD, be sure it's readily accessible; you may need it in a hurry.

The best compromise between safety and convenience is an inflatable PFD. When worn aboard a boat, an inflatable PFD doesn't impede your movement like bulkier PFDs, but in the water its built-in CO_2 canisters provide flotation at a moment's notice. (*A note for travelers:* Current airline regulations may preclude you from carrying or shipping CO_2 canisters on a plane. Check with your airline.)

Carry spare parts and a few tools on board the boat, especially if you're relying on an engine to get about. Shear pins on the propeller are

This angler has configured his canoe so he can cast from a sitting position. Note that he's also wearing an inflatable PFD.

notorious for breaking; you should know how to replace one and have a spare. A spark plug wrench is handy for removing and clearing a fouled plug, and you should have an extra paddle and an anchor.

Secure Everything

If you beach your canoe or boat, be sure to tie it securely to some immovable object, like a tree, or it may end up getting away from you. While fishing one night, a friend of mine left his inflatable boat on the beach, and several hours later it floated away with the tide, wind, and current. He still hasn't found it. Another time, my son and I were fishing from a canoe. We got out ever-so-briefly to land a nice brown trout. After removing the hook, I took a few extra moments to properly revive and release the fish. While our

Before You Set Off in a Boat

Here are three important tips to keep in mind as you prepare for a fishing trip by boat.

1. Always, always tell someone where you're going and when you're likely to return. Leave a float plan with a family member or close friend. If something happens and your return is delayed, the authorities can use the float plan to locate you.

2. Be sure to check the weather forecast before heading out. While the weather may be sunny and calm in the morning, the vagaries of wind, weather, and water can change an idyllic setting into a cauldron of hostility with one crack of thunder. The rule of thumb here is "Know before you go!"

3. A bathymetric map or chart of the lake, pond, or bay can help you navigate and also quickly orient you to likely fish holding areas. Look for these charts at your state fish and wildlife agency, tackle shop, or the local marina.

attention was focused on that lovely fish, neither my son nor I noticed that the canoe had drifted away. We found the boat about a hundred feet downstream, entangled in some trees along the opposite bank. I took off my chest waders and clothes and swam for it. My son still has the photo of me in wet briefs, paddling back upstream.

Your boat isn't the only thing that can get away from you. Tie all your spare gear, including your anchor, into the boat—even if it seems inconvenient to do so. Should your boat capsize, you'll have a better chance of recovering your stuff if it doesn't sink or float away. Lost gear ruins trips!

Casting Safety

It's possible to cast while standing in a small boat, but there is a higher risk of losing balance and toppling over. It's worthwhile to learn to cast from a seated position. It's not that different from casting on your feet; for the most part you just have to hold your casting arm a bit higher. At the last Boy Scout Jamboree, one fellow wanted to learn how to cast from his wheelchair. Because I know how to cast from a seated position, I was just as enthusiastic about teaching him as he was to learn. In a few moments, he was casting quite well.

When someone is in the boat with you, be careful with your backcast. Try to keep your backcast moving toward the outside of the boat and away from all passengers.

TIP: If the wind is blowing hard, you might want to pinch down the barb with your forceps or pliers or use barbless hooks. This will ease the removal of an errant hook from clothing, gear, or your guide's leg.

Fishing from Float Tubes and Kayaks

Float tubes are essentially a cross between a boat and an inner tube. Their light weight is their one big advantage. They can be backpacked into the high country very easily, inflated for use, and then deflated for the return trip. You propel the tube with swim fins on your feet. I also recommend taking a small, one-pound anchor (available at www.westmarine.com). An anchor will halt your drift and also keep the tube from floating away should you leave it for a moment. Always wear a PFD whenever you use a float tube.

There's no denying the growing popularity of fishing from kayaks. If this is a possibility that interests you, be sure to seek appropriate training in handling this special craft so that you know what to do in the event of an emergency.

TIP: If you see bad weather brewing, get off the water as soon as possible. Don't take any chances with boats and fast-developing weather.

Noise

Sound travels much faster and farther through water than through air, so any noise you make rapidly transfers to the fish. Sharp noises like a banging paddle, rattling anchor, or dropped pop bottle are not natural sounds, and they can alert a skittish fish to danger. Remember, when a fish senses danger, feeding stops!

Sounds will happen, however, even in the most disciplined boat. If the fish turns off because of sound, the best thing to do is "rest" it for a bit. In many cases, 10 to 15 minutes is all the fish needs before it resumes its normal feeding behavior. Perhaps this is a good time to quietly tie on another piece of tippet, change your fly, or have a snack. If you just want to enjoy the day, watch a bird, or merely view the scenery, those activities are OK, too! My grandfather's fishing buddy liked to "rest his fish" by taking a nap streamside in the warm afternoon sun!

HUR 19

SAFETY AND FIRST AID

Although fly-fishing may seem like a more benign sport than, say, football or skiing, it too has its share of accidents. I mean, think about it. Here's a sport in which we go into the wild, sometimes miles from civilization, and cast sharp hooks from what may be some pretty treacherous terrain: slippery rocks, rushing water, or perhaps a tippy boat. Add to those the vagaries of weather, the blazing sun, wild animals, and poison plants and there's plenty of opportunity for something bad to happen. Take precautions and be prepared.

Start with the Basics

I'm going to start right off by naming three must-haves on a fly-fishing trip: a good hat, quality polarized sunglasses, and appropriate sunscreen. Don't leave home without them! When hooks start to fly, nothing beats a good hat and protective eyewear as a first line of defense. We also know that overexposure to the sun can lead to skin cancer and eye disorders. That said, we can move on.

When I'm planning to go into the wilderness, my doctor suggests I stop taking my daily 81 mg dose of aspirin. Aspirin thins the blood; if you cut yourself, your blood may not clot quickly enough.

I always take along a small first-aid kit containing bandages, antiseptic, antihistamine, hydrocortisone cream, motion sickness pills, aspirin (despite my previous warning), and a short piece of strong fishing line to help remove imbedded hooks.

TIP: If you get a severe cut, your first priority is to stop the bleeding. If you have to, use duct tape to seal the wound and stop the bleeding. Keep the wound as clean as possible, and remember that a doctor can treat any infection later.

Hook Removal

When you're around hooks a lot, someone will eventually get hooked. If you're using a barbless hook, you merely have to back it out of the wound and treat the wound as you would any puncture wound. Barbed hooks, however, present a higher degree of difficulty. Fortunately, you can usually remove a hook that's embedded under the skin without the aid of a doctor.

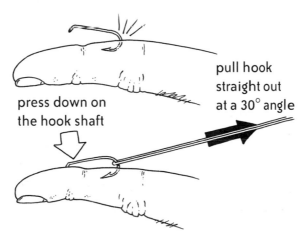

press down on
the hook shaft

pull hook
straight out
at a 30° angle

Hook removal technique.

In the past we would push the hook point up through the skin, cut off the barb, and then back the hook out of the wound. Now there's a simple hook removal technique that you can use to remove a hook quickly and safely. Please note that while it's possible to do this technique by yourself, it's easiest when performed with another person. Also note that you should never use this method to remove a hook from someone's eye. Instead, cover the eye with some gauze and seek medical attention as soon as possible. For most other bodily locations, this new technique is a breeze.

1. With strong string or a section of your fly line, make a loop around the bend of the hook.
2. With one hand, grasp both ends of the string firmly and securely. With the other hand, firmly press down on the hook's shaft to free the barb from the surrounding tissue.
3. While continuing to press down on the hook shank, quickly yank the string at about a 30-degree angle to pull the hook from the wound. The hook should come out the same hole in which it went.

Here are some hints that may make the job a little easier, safer, and more successful.

▸ Practice this technique on an orange or other piece of fruit or on an uncooked piece of chicken.
▸ Make sure the line you use is strong enough and won't break.
▸ Once you start to yank, continue to yank at the same angle in the same direction. Don't jerk the line forward and then back; no double pumps.
▸ The hook will come out quickly, so make sure no one is standing behind you.
▸ After the removal, apply a local antiseptic to the wound and check with your doctor to ensure your tetanus shot is still current.
▸ When I'm removing a hook from someone else, I like to tell the patient that I'll pull on the count of three, then I pull on two instead, before he or she can tense up.

If you're still unsure about removing a hook on your own, use a suitable bandage to protect the wound and immobilize the hook, then seek appropriate medical attention.

Bear Safety

When it comes to fishing and bears, my philosophy is that a day without a bear sighting is a good day of fishing. This goes for moose as well. Too many people believe the Disney version of the wild kingdom; that large wild animals benignly avoid humans. Those of us who know better see large wild animals for what they really are: large wild animals. They can be very unpredictable, so it's best to avoid them whenever possible. It certainly isn't in your best interest to attract them, so adhere to all campsite rules regarding food storage and camp cleanliness.

TIP: Do not bring food into your tent. Animals have a great sense of smell, so even sealed containers may not provide adequate protection. Wash all dirty dishes and discard or burn all food scraps. Leaving food around your campsite only invites trouble. If you're in bear country, you may have to suspend your food from high tree branches.

In bear country, it's wise to carry a large canister of bear spray. In Alaska, for example, there has never been a documented case in which someone using bear spray according to the manufacturer's instructions has been killed by a bear. Unfortunately, there have been numerous cases in which people were killed when they used firearms as their sole protection.

When moving through bear country, it's OK to make noise as you walk down the trail. Talking, singing, or ringing bells are fine ways to do this. If you see a bear coming your way, bunch up with the other members of your party and try to look as big as possible. Again, in Alaska there has never

When bears get this close to you, it's time to move on. Mama Bear is not too far away.

been a documented case in which a brown bear has attacked a group of three or more people.

If you're fighting a fish and a bear approaches, break off the fish (cut your line) immediately and back slowly away from the bear. If you have a stringer of fish, leave it behind; that's probably what the bear is most interested in anyway.

Finally, if you're attacked by a brown bear, roll onto your stomach, keep your backpack on, and cover your head with your hands. If the bear tries to roll you over, get back onto your stomach.

If you're attacked by a black bear, you would do just the opposite: fight back by kicking and punching the bear as best you can.

All this comes back to what I said earlier: a day without a bear sighting is a good day of fishing!

Other Safety Precautions

Electricity

A graphite fly rod will conduct electricity. Do not try to play Ben Franklin when there is an electrical storm in the area. Get off the water and seek shelter. On a trip to the Bahamas, I waited a whole day before the tide was right and the bonefish were tailing. I mean, they were just about everywhere. Nonetheless, a fast-approaching thunderstorm overpowered my temptation to stay. I may have been disappointed, but I was safe and lived to tell the tale. No fish is worth your life!

Similarly, when you're practicing casting, make sure there are no electrical wires overhead.

If you see a storm brewing, get off the water. Don't take any chances with fast-developing weather. Carbon fly rods will conduct electricity, and you don't want to be the highest spot around.

Burns

Burns are most likely to occur at the campsite when preparing meals or relaxing beside a campfire. Also be careful around fuel and hot engines. First-degree burns—characterized by reddening of the skin—happen when something very hot briefly touches your skin. Simply immerse the affected area in cold or ice water. Doing so usually takes the sting out, and then you can bandage the burn if it's warranted. Second- and third-degree burns—characterized respectively by blistering and more severe tissue damage—happen when there is prolonged exposure to heat or flame and require professional medical attention. Keep second- and third-degree burns clean, cover them with suitable dressings, and get the victim to a medical facility as soon as possible.

Insect Bites

It's a natural fact: wherever you find fish, you'll also find biting bugs. It seems that the more fish there are, the more bugs there are, too. We anglers have to live with this truth and adapt accordingly. While many bug bites are harmless, there appears to be an increasing number of aggressive diseases, such as Lyme disease, West Nile virus, and Eastern equine encephalitis, carried by bugs. These diseases can be severely debilitating, if not fatal. Your best defense is to wear protective clothing and insect repellant. If you're sleeping in a tent, zip up the insect screens quickly as you enter and leave. Keep the bugs outside where they belong.

If you do get a bug bite and experience symptoms other than the normal transient itching and swelling, see your doctor. Watch for flu-like symptoms and rashes. If possible, capture the bug and bring it to your doctor for subsequent identification and analysis. This protocol is especially important if you're bitten by a spider or a tick.

Animal Bites

Take wild animal bites very seriously; report all bites to your doctor, no matter how minor. Wild critters carry all sorts of germs including brucellosis, tularemia, and rabies. Don't feed wild animals or attract them to your camp. Even a cute chipmunk, squirrel, or mouse can pass along some nasty diseases.

Snakes, like spiders, eat lots of pests and should be considered one of the "good guys." For the most part, snakes will try to avoid humans. If you do encounter one, give it a way to escape and let it go on its way. If a snake bites you, however, proceed as you would with any other wild animal bite: seek immediate medical attention, especially if the snake is poisonous.

Poisonous Plants

Those of us who are allergic to poison ivy know that white berries and three shiny leaves are the warning signs to look for, and we avoid touching the plant. (Note that poison sumac and poison oak also have white berries.) Poison ivy can take many different forms ranging from a ground-dwelling vine to a large shrub to a tree-like form. Be sure you can identify all of them, especially if you're allergic.

Obviously, when dealing with poisonous plants, the best first aid is to simply avoid touching them. If you have touched them, wash away the poisonous resin with lots of soap and water as quickly as possible.

Drinking Water

The guidelines for avoiding illness from drinking water are simple. Drink water from safe sources only. Never drink untreated or unfiltered water from a lake, stream, river, or pond. Water needs to be boiled for 3 to 10 minutes, chemically treated, or filtered to remove or kill most common bacteria and viruses. Diseases like giardiasis are very common in the wild and can be a terrible and painful way to lose weight!

HOUR 20

EXPANDING YOUR FLY-FISHING HORIZONS

One huge attraction of fly-fishing is the wonderful opportunities it offers for adventure and travel. While you may improve your fishing skills around home, almost everyone I know also enjoys taking these skills elsewhere, too. Saltwater fishing or fishing in far-away countries are just two ways that fly-fishing can engender adventure.

Saltwater Fly-Fishing

Saltwater fly-fishing is the fastest-growing segment of the sport. Since most of our population lives on or near the coast, fishing in salt water is a natural fit. Saltwater fly-fishing also makes a great deal of sense when you consider that the action may slow down in many freshwater fishing haunts on hot summer days. Striped bass, bluefish, bonito, snook, permit, tarpon, bonefish, drum, and sea trout are some of the most sought-after saltwater species. These fish are generally bigger and more powerful than their freshwater cousins, and they're accessible. You can actually catch large saltwater predators from the docks that line many of our coastal cities.

Saltwater Gear

The bigger water requires bigger gear. To help you successfully land larger, more powerful fish, you'll need a larger rod with less flex and more strength than the 5- or 6-weight fly rod you use back home. An 8- or 9-weight rod will allow you to land and release these bigger fish quicker. (If you plan on catching even larger fish like tarpon or marlin, even heavier rods are warranted.)

To use a heavier rod, you need to match the fly line to the rod weight; for example, with an 8- or 9-weight rod you would use an 8- or 9-weight fly line. I like a sinking-tip line in water deeper than 8 feet and a floating line

A saltwater rod and a bonefish.

in shallower water. Also, although fifty yards of backing may suffice in fresh water, one hundred to two hundred yards is more appropriate in salt water. The change in fly line, of course, means you need a larger, saltwater-protected reel with a smooth-running drag system.

If you're seeking toothy predators, tie a short steel leader near the hook. This can help prevent the fish from chewing up your monofilament leader and breaking free. Some anglers use a stripping basket to help keep stripped fly line organized and under control between casts. A stripping basket is a container you wear around your waist. As you strip fly line from the water, the line collects in the basket. When you cast, the fly line in the basket is pulled outward. A stripping basket works really well when you're standing in fast-moving current, or if you don't want to accidentally step on the fly line, or when a hooked fish is making its first strong run away from you.

A stripping basket around your waist will help keep your fly line under control.

Flies for Saltwater Fishing

Saltwater flies are constructed somewhat differently than their freshwater counterparts. Saltwater fish generally pursue larger prey than freshwater fish, so the fly may have to be bigger to match the size of the prey species. Also, because seawater is corrosive, the hooks are often sea-guarded or made of stainless steel. The materials used to construct these flies often have flamboyant colors and lots of reflective Mylar. Eyes are often a big part of a saltwater fly, as some predators key in on eye size when they seek something to eat.

In salt water, I like Clousers and Deceivers in various shades and sizes. White and chartreuse, black, and barred are most effective. I also like to add a little red—often by merely using red fly-tying thread—as this color seems to provoke the most strikes. Clousers and Deceivers mimic

An assortment of saltwater flies.

smaller fish. If you're fishing for bonefish or some other shrimp-eating fish, Crazy Charlies—particularly in pink—are also consistently effective.

There are many other saltwater patterns, including squid and crabs, both of which can be indispensable when fish are feeding on those critters. The point is, when you're starting out, old standby patterns like these will work just fine. If you look up local fishing reports for the area where you plan to fish, these same patterns will be mentioned time and again. They're common because, well, they catch fish.

Where to Find Fish

Some likely spots to fish for saltwater species include the mouths of inlets or tidal rivers where, during tide changes, the water flows like a fresh-water river. Predators seem to concentrate in areas where a strong current can be disadvantageous to smaller prey.

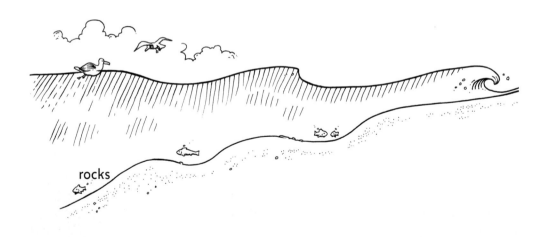

estuary or bay

Fish can be found in the waters where a river enters a bay or estuary. You can also fish around rock piles, trees, or other structures.

TIP: As you would in fresh water, cast over and across the mouths of inlets or tidal rivers, mend, and allow your fly to sweep downstream.

On shallow coastal flats, move slowly, wear subdued colors, be quiet, and look for any signs of fish passing. Often the color of the fish matches the color of the bottom, so you might only see a shadow or a slight movement. Wearing polarized sunglasses is a must. When you finally spot a fish, estimate where it's heading, and present your fly about 15 to 20 feet in front of it. Shallow-water fish are the most easily spooked fish of all. If something doesn't seem right to them, they're outta there!

With your fly, explore any submerged rocks or rock structures like jetties, groins, breakwaters, or seawalls. Baitfish are attracted to such

At dusk or dawn, fish often patrol the shallow areas near shore. Move slowly and carefully, and cast your fly near the closest rocks first, then a bit farther out.

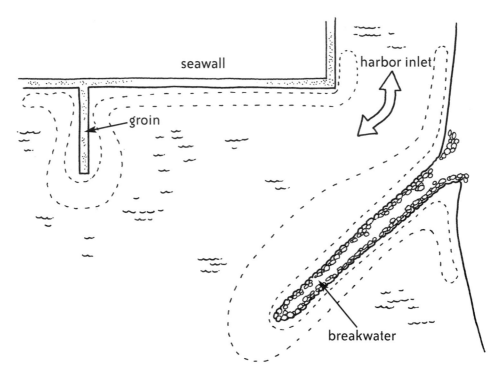

Fish from groins, seawalls, and breakwaters, particularly in early morning or evening when the current is moving. Watch out for slippery rocks.

places because they offer cover and food items. Predators will often move into these areas, too. The turbulent water caused by waves crashing over rocks provides a distinct advantage for predators. Remember: larger fish can swim better in current than small ones, so larger fish will seek out these areas to exploit their swimming advantage. If there is current creating additional turbulence around a structure, so much the better. Be there in the early morning or at dusk and be ready.

Beaches, too, can make for good fishing. Look carefully along what may appear to be a flat sandy beach; you might spot a trough just behind the surf zone that runs parallel to the beach. Large predators looking for a meal often cruise these slightly deeper channels in search of any smaller fish swimming in light to moderate surf. To reach the channel, cast your fly about ten feet or more over the backside of a wave as it breaks.

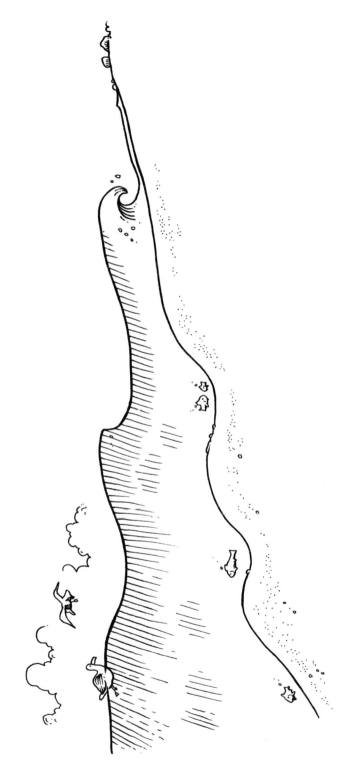

A coastal beach often will have a series of sand troughs that are formed by breaking waves. These troughs run parallel to the beach and serve as pathways for fish to move about and feed.

When you arrive on a beach, look along the surf line for signs of rising fish or diving sea birds. Approach the water slowly, and keep as low as possible. The fish will often move back and forth along the beach, so you might not have to chase them; just wait, and they'll come back.

If birds are feeding from the surf, it's likely that predator fish are forcing baitfish toward the water's surface. Birds have great vision and can see this potential surface feast from a distance. As more birds gather, the predators squeeze the baitfish from below while the birds squeeze them from above. Baitfish fly out of the water to avoid being eaten by underwater predators, and these predators leap out of the water in fast pursuit. The gulls dive into the mix with abandon. Watching such a feeding frenzy, in which nature is at its best and worst, is quite exciting.

So where do you fit into this picture? If you can just get any fly into the maelstrom you'll catch something, so hang on! And I guarantee that you'll forget the pile of paperwork stacked on your desk. Your problem at the moment is to get off another cast without hooking yourself or your companion or otherwise getting your hook fouled. With all that's going on around you, try to remain calm. Work slowly, and make that perfect cast. I know: easier said than done!

Docks can provide excellent saltwater fishing. When fishing from a dock, look for big swirls in the water or gulls or terns diving from above. Some docks will have overhead lights, and if it's legal to do so, fishing in the evening under those lights is a great way to catch fish. The lights bring up plankton the same way a flame attracts moths. Little fish come to eat the plankton, and larger fish come to eat the little fish. If you're really lucky, a giant of a predator will sweep through, and if you just have your fly in the right spot, at the right moment, life is sweet!

Saltwater Fishing Safety

Although many of the same safety and first aid issues related to freshwater fishing apply to saltwater fishing (see Hour 19), we can't leave the subject of saltwater fishing without giving its unique safety issues a nod. Rocks found in salt water can be especially slippery; waves, wind, and tidal currents can be unforgiving; and saltwater hooks—due to their size and weight—can really hurt. Often the pace of saltwater fishing itself can be very fast and exciting. Enjoy the moment, but always have a little part of your brain tuned in to common sense and safety. If you hook a fish with large teeth, use pliers to remove the hook; a fish out of water can still give you a nasty bite. And don't take any unnecessary chances, as no fish is worth you or someone else getting hurt.

Fly-Fishing for Freshwater Species Other than Trout

According to the most current statistics compiled by the U.S. Fish and Wildlife Service, about 34 million anglers fish a total of 557 million days annually in the United States. Of these, almost 8 million anglers like to fish for trout, although not all of them fish with flies. Additionally, more than 10 million anglers fish for black bass, a group of fish that includes smallmouth bass, largemouth bass, and spotted bass. Even fewer bass anglers, however, use fly rods. This is unfortunate, as they're missing a great challenge and experience. Catching a big bass on a dry fly is a real kick.

A Closer Look at Smallmouth and Largemouth Bass

Smallmouth bass are fantastic leapers, so when you hook one, hold on! Like rainbow trout, smallmouth bass often leap from the water several times before you get them to the net. Although you can generally find them in rivers, they're also quite common in lakes and reservoirs. They readily take dry flies and nymphs. When bass are establishing their spawning area, they're extremely vulnerable to a big deer-hair fly, like a Stimulator, and will aggressively charge it. The Clouser minnow was first developed to catch smallmouth bass, so it's an obvious choice. But, really, when you get right down to it, catching one of these fish on a 5- or 6-weight fly rod with any fly can be great fun.

Largemouth bass is another great fish species to catch on a fly rod. Although they will take larger flies, I once caught a world-record largemouth (8.8 lb. on 4 lb. test) on a size 8 Woolly Bugger. A largemouth bass caught on a fly rod can be an extremely persistent fighter as well as a powerful adversary. Old Bucket Mouth can really give you a thrill as it leaps from the water, shaking its head wildly in an effort to rid itself of the fly. It will also make powerful runs and try to get you entangled in a bramble. Don't overlook the opportunity to try to catch one.

TIP: If a largemouth bass heads toward a bramble, use your rod leverage to steer it into open water where you have a chance of landing this hog.

Other Species of Freshwater Fish

There are many other freshwater fish species that are readily accessible to most fishers who want to stretch beyond trout fishing. If you only go trout fishing, you likely won't be fishing as much, and that's just not good. Let's face it: every hour of fishing only adds more quality to your life!

Many freshwater anglers will tell you that the first fish they ever caught was a sunfish. A lake or pond with a large sunfish, bream, or similar warm-water fish population is a great place to practice your casting and hook-setting techniques. You can gain a lot of fly-fishing experience by catching forty to fifty bluegill in an hour or two. These fish readily take small dry flies and poppers, and they're deceptively great fighters for their size. You can release them unharmed, and they have a great rate of recovery. In fact, you may even catch the same fish more than once in the same afternoon.

Other species of note include black and white crappie. Noted for their good taste, these fish can often be found near any kind of structure—brush piles, rock piles, and the like—in many lakes and ponds. If you find one fish, you likely will find many more in the same area, and they will readily take nymphs and Woolly Buggers.

Pond shiners and fallfish will take dry flies off the water's surface. They will assuredly test your fly presentation skills. White and yellow perch can give you quite a bit of action. Walleye, one of the best-eating freshwater fish species, are aggressive attackers of larger streamer flies. Fish for them in the evening when the light is fading and the fish are moving closer to the surface.

Northern pike, pickerel, and muskellunge are all from the same family of fish and all are ferocious predators with formidable teeth. Fishing for these fighting species requires baitfish imitations and steel leaders. Also, these fish can grow quite large and can be every bit as powerful as some of the coastal species. When you catch one, be sure to use pliers to remove the hook; those needle-sharp teeth can give you some nasty cuts.

Last but not least, don't overlook the common carp. If you know where there is a mulberry tree overhanging the water, go there when the berries are falling and have a mulberry imitation fly ready. When you catch one of these steamrolling fish, be prepared for the long haul. Carp just don't seem to run out of gas and will fight for a long time before tiring. I guarantee that if you hook a big one, your arms will get a good workout.

Where to Find More Information

I'm sure there are numerous other species of freshwater fish common to your area. Contact your state district fishery biologist and ask for information on where to go and what to look for. Fishery biologists continue to do lake, river, stream, and pond surveys, and they're the most up-to-date source of information. Some can even give you specific hints on access points and the best flies to use. Ask if pond contour maps are available, as they can help you find drop-offs, structure, or prominences where fish are likely to hold.

Remember, though, that your goal is to go fishing and relax. Who knows? Maybe once in a while you'll even be rewarded with a delicious fish.

Fishing in Foreign Lands

Fishing is a great excuse to travel to places you might not otherwise consider. Traveling also offers you an opportunity to enjoy your favorite season virtually all year long. When it's snowing out your back door, slip out the front and head to the airport. After a few hours of flying time, you can be at a new fishing hole, in short sleeves and chest waders, casting your first fly.

Speaking of Language

Although English speakers can be found in major cities throughout the world, learning the native language of a foreign country—even if only the most basic skill level—will increase your enjoyment of the culture, provide more opportunities to get meals for yourself, and give you enhanced independence to move around. Don't be fearful of making mistakes. The effort, even if a bit stilted, will be greatly appreciated and welcomed by the folks who live there. Also, your confidence will increase the more you use the language. Don't wait, however, until the last minute to learn basic vocabulary.

It doesn't matter where in the world you are: if you check with your outfitter, you'll find you can pretty much use the same equipment and flies that you use at home. Here, an angler will cast a bushy dry fly into the faster-moving water of a New Zealand river.

Outfitters and Foreign Guides

Fishing for foreign fish species can be great sport. Who can deny the fun of catching your first peacock bass, South American dorado, bonefish, or permit. Ask your outfitter what kinds of flies or other specialized gear you might need. If you don't bring it with you, you might learn that it's almost impossible to find at your distant fishing destination.

If you plan to hire a guide, be sure to inquire about language skills beforehand. Many guides in the outback will have a limited English vocabulary, so communication may be reduced to hand signals and facial gestures. Although some people may find this problem comical and fun, it can easily become extremely frustrating and time-consuming in the long run.

Be aware that many rural guides still smoke. If this is an issue, be sure to discuss it with your outfitter before you head out for the day.

Mention any special dietary requirements that you have. These people really want to please you, but if you surprise them with last-minute special requests in remote areas, they may not be able to help. Make arrangements beforehand or bring the stuff with you.

Preparing for International Travel

All countries will require you to go through immigration or customs during the entry process. For the most part, the process is simple and easy if you follow directions.

Because of invasive aquatic pests like zebra mussels, algae, and the New Zealand mud snail—all known to hitchhike about the world on our wading shoes—you should take steps to sanitize fishing equipment prior to departure. These living, invasive pests can be even more destructive than simple trash, because once they enter a habitat, they're almost impossible to eradicate. The problem is serious, and customs officials do not fool around. By cleaning and sanitizing your gear, you'll be practicing Leave-No-Trace practices on a biological level.

Pack sharp tools like a Leatherman multitool in your checked luggage. Compressed gas containers like carbon dioxide cartridges or butane cigarette lighters may be prohibited anywhere on the airplane—in carry-on bags and checked luggage. Additional restrictions may exist, so you are encouraged to contact your carrier or the Transportation Security Administration (www.tsa.gov) to determine the current restricted items.

Dealing with Travel-Related Discomforts

I don't quite know how it works, but jet lag always seems to be most apparent when you return home, regardless of whether you travel east or west. My rule of thumb is it takes about a day to acclimate to each

Passports, Money, and Other Practical Matters

A reputable travel guide will provide comprehensive information about what and what not to do when traveling to or in a particular country. Here is a short list of some practical matters to bear in mind when planning a trip to a foreign land.

Passport. Always know the whereabouts of your passport. If you accidentally lose it, report immediately to the nearest passport-issuing embassy.

Traveler's Checks and Credit Cards. Having internationally recognized traveler's checks, some cash, and at least one major credit card should be adequate for you to get around. See if your credit card company imposes currency conversion charges. If so, consider finding a card that's more tourist-friendly. Personally, I use my credit card for most of my overseas purchases, including lodging, because it gives me the best available exchange rate.

Cash. You need to have a little cash to cover small purchases, taxis, local transportation, and gratuities. Some smaller hotels may only take cash. Also, several countries assess an exit fee when you leave, so keep some local currency available just for this purpose.

Bargaining. The natives in some countries may consider it an insult if you don't bargain with them. Check with the locals to determine the appropriate practice.

Crime. Don't flash cash, and keep your wealth hidden. If you own a Rolex watch, great, but consider leaving it at home and taking a Timex with you instead. Also, in countries with high crime rates, having a throw-away wallet containing a few dollars and some inconsequential ID cards might satisfy a passing thief.

Gifts. If I'm planning to meet anyone in a foreign country, I always bring along a few gifts. One of my favorites is maple syrup because it's not readily available in other countries. I call this gesture Maple Syrup Diplomacy because most people enjoy the sweet taste, and if the gesture conjures up positive thoughts about a few traveling Americans, perhaps the world is a bit better off.

time zone you cross, no matter which direction you're traveling. If you travel to Alaska from the East Coast, for example, it may take you 4 to 5 days to fully adjust to the Alaskan time. Rest well and avoid caffeine and alcohol.

TIP: Consult your physician before international travel and long flights. In addition to making simple suggestions that may make your traveling experience more comfortable, he or she may offer prescriptions to combat diarrhea or severe bacterial infections and recommend inoculations to protect you in the countries you wish to visit.

Food and water can pose a bit of a problem in foreign countries. To avoid food poisoning, make sure all meat and other food is fully cooked and served hot. Unless you're assured otherwise, avoid fresh salad, as it may have been washed in contaminated water. While it probably won't kill you, you may have to take several additional potty breaks during the day and lose valuable fishing time. Drink only bottled water and drinks, which are available just about everywhere in the world.

Trip and Auto Insurance

There are companies that offer trip insurance to protect you from losses, should you not be able to travel for a covered reason like a medical problem. Some companies will pick you up, no matter where you are, and fly you out of the fishing area to a modern hospital of your choice. Without trip insurance, the out-of-pocket cost of evacuation can be many thousands of dollars.

If you're a victim of any crime or are involved in an automobile accident in a foreign country, you need to report it to both your embassy and the local authorities. Check with your insurance company before you head overseas to determine if your existing auto insurance will cover you. They'll advise you on alternatives if it doesn't.

If you fish in New Zealand, you may see some gargantuan old trees along the riverbank. Is that a hobbit sneaking through there? No, just the author.

As you move about the world on your fishing expeditions, embrace the unexpected. You'll make new discoveries. You'll have adventures. Each experience will be a personal treasure. Be sure to record these memories with a reliable camera. With Internet cafes almost everywhere now, you can download digital photographs and speed them to your friends and family within seconds. With a satellite phone, you can call home from any spot on the planet. Let there be no doubt that in this modern age, the world is small and becoming smaller with each new technological advance.

The fish, however, have stayed pretty consistent no matter where they are; they still want to rise to a simple fly, and you'll want to be the one offering it. Some things just don't change, no matter what's happening in the world.

Time Check

We've covered a lot of ground so far. I wouldn't be surprised if you've already gone out there and caught a few fish. If you have, bravo! If not, perhaps you're waiting to tie a few flies of your own first. We have just enough time to tie four flies, and still meet our 24-hour goal.

H☉URS 21–24

AN INTRODUCTION TO FLY TYING

Aldo Leopold, one of the world's leading conservationists, once wrote that double is the pleasure of those who catch fish on flies they themselves have tied. I encourage you to take up this part of the sport if for no other reason than to help you pass away the winter months when fly-fishing is difficult or impossible.

TIP: I view flies and fly tying as an impressionistic art form. It's not what *you* think the fly looks like, but rather what the fish sees.

In day-to-day fishing, the ability to tie your own flies will be a great advantage. If, for example, you see fish selectively rising to a certain bug, you can tie a similar pattern at home that evening, and be ready to use it the next day. There are anglers who will tie the fly right there on the stream bank. The point is, although a few flies will address most situations on most days, there will be times when you'll need additional patterns in your fly box. Your ability to tie flies will help you catch more fish. If you can figure out what they're eating, you can tie a suitable imitation and set yourself up for a wonderful day of fishing.

A Word on Fly Patterns

Select any fly-tying book, or go to www.hookhack.com/flypatterns.html. You can be sure these resources will include recipes for the construction, or *dressing*, of all sorts of flies. By using the recommended ingredients you'll create a fly that will be recognized throughout the fly-fishing community. Many flies have evolved to their current patterns because they've proved successful. If you make any changes to the recipe, the fly may be less attractive to fish. In other words, when it comes to tying flies, it's best to stay with the tried and true. As you gain more fly-tying experience, you too can develop and test your own patterns. When you design a pattern that's clearly successful, share it with other anglers by submitting it for publication. But for now, simply try to learn a few basic, traditional patterns.

TIP: When someone gives you a fly, put it into a large fly box. I call mine the library. Then use the fly as a model for tying copies of that pattern. If you use the fly instead or, worse, lose the original, you may never remember the subtle structure that's integral to that fly's success.

The first rule of fly tying is *never tie just one fly of a particular pattern.* Always tie two or more. Invariably, the day you find a fly that works, you'll lose it. This is especially true when tying a prototype pattern. One morning several years back, a buddy and I were fishing at a small lake just a few miles from my home. At sunrise, my buddy started to catch fish, one right after the other. Meanwhile, I was standing about thirty feet away from him and didn't get so much as a bite. After about thirty minutes, I finally asked what fly he was using. He told me he'd just tied the fly the night before and it was falling apart. Sure enough, by the time I saw the fly it consisted of some thread, some unraveled feathers, and not much else. We called it the Morning Glory. But because he'd tied only one, this great pattern is now extinct! Although he tried, he could never duplicate the original.

Equipment and Materials

As is true of most art forms, you'll need equipment. After all, the Impressionists couldn't work without their palettes and brushes, right? Here are the items a fly tier can't live without.

Vise

The first piece you'll need is a vise. Vises come in many makes and models, some of which are downright ingenious. Remember, a lot of brilliant people have devoted much of their brainpower to catch a fish with a fly. Some of these people may be highly skilled engineers or machinists by day, but after-hours they become obsessed with designing and building the best mousetrap, or fly-tying vise.

Look for a vise that has hardened steel jaws. A vise's jaws exert a lot of pressure on hooks, and over time jaws that are made out of softer metal may deform and lose their holding power. Also, look for a vise that's fully adjustable—you'll need it to hold many different sizes of hooks.

Although I like vises by Regal, Abel, Griffin, HMH, and Dyna-King, my personal favorite is the Cam Traveler—an affordable rotary vise by Renzetti. A rotary vise has a handle that allows you rotate the fly such that you can work on the top or underside of the fly. This feature is especially useful when tying matched components like wings on either side of the fly. Is it absolutely necessary to have a rotary vise? No. But they can make fly tying easier, especially when you begin dressing complex patterns.

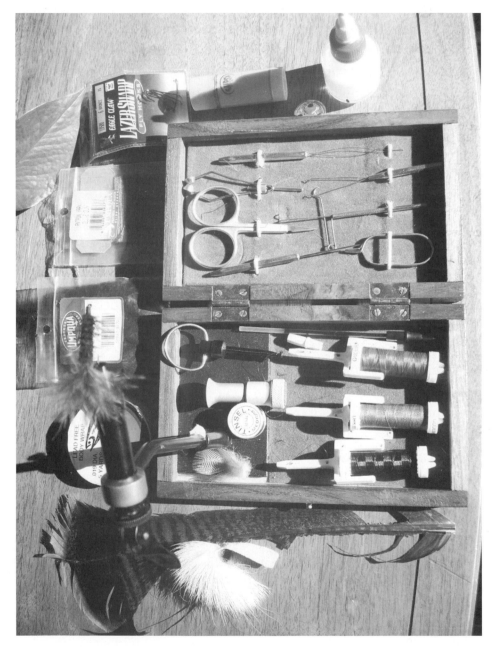

A Royal Coachman Tool Kit and assorted fly-tying materials.

While I generally recommend the best vise you can afford, for travel I particularly like my Royal Coachman standard tool kit (contact www.cabelas.com or www.harelinedubbing.com to find the nearest dealer). This unit comes in a compact wooden box. In it you'll find a built-in pedestal vise and the tools you need to tie most flies. It's also small enough to take streamside for those times when you need to tie just the right fly. While this nonrotary vise may not be made of the highest-quality steel, it should give you several years of service if you don't abuse it. The cost (about $25 at the time of this writing) is so reasonable you may want to get one of these kits to serve as your primary vise until you can afford something better and more versatile. I stuff my kit with hooks and any materials I think I'll need. Back in the days when you were allowed to bring scissors on planes, I would even tie flies on my way to a fishing trip.

Small Tools

SCISSORS

Scissors are another tool you don't want to skimp on. Buy quality scissors, and keep them sharp.

TIP: Cut fine materials with the tips of your scissors, cut coarser materials like feather shafts with the blade centers, and cut thin-gauge wire at the base.

HACKLE PLIERS

Hackle pliers are used to hold fly-tying material in places where your fingers don't seem to fit. You can choose from a broad selection of hackle pliers, and as long as they firmly hold feathers and hackle without breaking them, I'm happy. E-Z Hackle Pliers, a spring-loaded type available from Cabelas, come in handy for tying the four-twist loop, so you may want to purchase a few of these.

The Ubiquitous BIC Pen: A Cheap Fly-Tying Tool

When you complete a fly, you don't have to use the whip-finishing tool that many fly tiers use. It takes a bit of practice to use one, and there is a much simpler method of securing the thread when you complete a fly. Tie about six half hitches and coat them with fly tying cement and your fly should hold together fairly well. (For detailed directions on how to tie a half hitch, see Step 11 of the Woolly Bugger tying instructions on page 213.)

You can make several tools for tying half hitches simply by taking apart a BIC pen. The tapered end of the outer casing that secures the ink stylus should fit over bead heads. Among the other disassembled parts of the pen, there are other hollow ends of various sizes, including the ink tube itself that can be used to tie half hitches on smaller flies.

HAIR STACKER

When you cut a small amount of hair from a hide, the tips of the hair will not be even. Using the hair this way may cause the fly to be unbalanced and may appear unnatural to a fish. A hair stacker allows you to align the tips prior to tying them into a fly. Turn to page 216 to see how a hair stacker is used.

TIP: When you cut a bunch of hair from a hide, cut as close to the skin as possible. By doing so you eliminate the need to remove half-cut hair stubs from future clippings. This is especially helpful when cutting hair clumps from tails. Also, when you need just the guard hairs, you can comb out the soft underfur with a tiny eyebrow or mustache comb.

BOBBIN

A bobbin holds the spool of fly-tying thread and is used to pay out thread as you need it. There are many good ones to choose from. Many flytiers use several bobbins, each containing a different color or gauge of thread. (Turn to page 209 to see how a bobbin is used.)

Most beginning flytiers haven't developed a sense of how much force to exert on the thread when dressing a fly. Obviously you want the thread to be taut, but not so tight that it breaks. The thread seems to break less often on bobbins that have a flexible tip. With time you'll get the feel of what is just the right amount of tension to apply.

A Butler GUM Eez-Thru dental floss threader makes a great bobbin threader. They're ultra-cheap and available at your local pharmacy.

BODKIN

A bodkin is a needle-like tool used to tease out small materials or to apply a small amount of head cement.

DUBBING TOOL

A dubbing tool is used to make a twisted dubbing rope to brush hair fibers so they bristle. This tool will be useful, for example, in creating the thorax of the Hare's Mask Nymph (see pages 227 and 228).

Fly-Tying Materials

To get started in fly tying, you'll need materials in addition to tools. One option is to buy a fly-tying kit that includes both tools and materials. Generally, the materials you'll find in fly-tying kits will be sufficient to tie basic patterns. As your interest in fly-tying grows, you can purchase more exotic materials for more intricate flies. You can also explore some other sources for fly-tying materials: hunters may have a supply of furs and feathers; second-hand clothing stores may have old fur garments; or fly-tying pals may be willing to share or trade some materials.

Another option is to buy a tool kit and materials separately. I recommend the Royal Coachman tool kit, a low-cost kit that comes with the fly-tying tools you need, including a portable pedestal vise but does not include fur, fibers, feathers, thread, and hooks.

TIP: Avoid using roadkill as a source of fly-tying materials. Such sources may carry diseases like rabies, and taking dead mammals and birds sometimes poses legal issues. The Migratory Bird Treaty Act prevents the possession of any migratory bird or its parts without a permit. Wild duck feathers are OK if taken legally, but they cannot be sold. Some feathers, like bald and golden eagles, are even more tightly restricted and only Native Americans can possess them without a USFWS permit. Some states also restrict taking road-killed fur animals if they're out of season.

HACKLE

Bird feathers that are used to dress your flies are called *hackle*. You can't go wrong with brands like Whiting, Metz, Keough, or Hoffman. These feathers come from chickens that are bred specifically for their quality feathers.

FUR

Your material kit should have a hare's mask and some elk or deer hair. Fur is composed of stiffer, shiny guard hairs—ideal for tail filaments—and a fine, softer underfur that can be used as dubbing (see below). Also try to get a woodchuck tail or some stiff bristles from a black chicken feather as a substitute. As you progress in fly tying, you'll want to add other types of fur or hair to your collection, such as caribou, woodchuck, squirrel tail, possum, badger, fox, moose mane, mink, black bear, muskrat, and the pink underbelly fur of a coyote.

DUBBING

Dubbing is a fine-textured material that you twist onto thread to make it just a bit fatter. The fatter thread is then used to simulate, for example, an insect body of a specific shape or color. I like to use natural underfur or belly fur when possible, but synthetics are readily available and come in lots of different colors. Umpqua Feather Merchants carries a synthetic product called ultra-fine dubbing. It also comes in a multicolor pack called a Dubbin-izer. Ultra-fine dubbing is easier to use than other kinds of synthetic dubbing and makes the thinnest dubbing "rope" or "brush."

HOOKS

The shapes and sizes of hooks are seemingly limitless. To keep things simple, use the size and brand that's recommended in each fly recipe.

I do suggest, however, that you buy quality hooks. Lesser-quality hooks may be brittle, out of shape, made with wire that's too heavy or too light, or may be relatively dull. In gardening, you don't skimp on seeds, and in house painting you don't buy cheap paint. Good hooks are ultimately the cheapest component of all the fly-tying materials, so it won't hurt to splurge.

TIP: Refer to www.hookhack.com for a manufacturer's hook conversion chart that will allow you to cross-reference and compare hook sizes from one brand to another. The website also offers a list of many hints for the fly-tying angler.

THREAD

Thread holds the fly together, and it's available in various sizes and colors. Fly-tying thread generally is flat and waxed, so it's a bit different from common sewing thread. Gudebrod makes some of the best thread around for every fly-tying need. Most freshwater flies in sizes 10 through 16 require size 6/0 thread. Fine threads like sizes 8/0 and 10/0 are used for really small hooks. If you're just getting started, 6/0 thread in black, brown, olive, red, and tan should suffice, although you'll want additional colors later on. For saltwater flies, you'll need heavier thread sizes like 3/0 to G, and black, chartreuse, red, yellow, and pink are excellent colors to get you started.

STORING YOUR MATERIALS

As you bring new natural materials into your collection, be sure to keep them isolated in tightly sealed plastic bags. Place a mothball or two in each bag to prevent potential problems with insects or other pests. Nothing is as destructive to your materials as a moth or insect larvae infestation, especially if it gets into your collection of $60 chicken neck feathers!

A Few Fly-Tying Tips

Before we begin tying, I'd like to offer a few general tips that will help make the work a little easier.

- **Tie the fly on a larger hook the first time.** When tying a pattern for the first time, use a larger-than-recommended hook. Doing so may give you a clearer understanding of the fly's scale and proportion. If you start too small too soon, you may run into problems that will be harder to resolve because of the smaller dimensions.
- **It's OK to make corrections as you go.** If you're not satisfied with the fly you're tying, don't hesitate to unwrap whatever section is bothering you. If necessary, use a razor blade to cut everything off the hook and start the fly over again. Keep practicing until you get it right.
- **Aim toward tying the perfect fly.** While you may not need to make a perfect fly each time, you should strive to do your best. Be your most exacting critic. As the quality of your flies improves, so will your catch rate.
- **Place the hook in the vise correctly.** Place the hook horizontally in the vise so the tip is on the bottom. The jaws of the vise should clamp down on the lower bend of the hook just as the hook begins to straighten out toward the barb. You know you have the vise adjusted correctly when the hook emits a "boing" sound when you pluck the eye and the hook hasn't changed position. (Refer to any photo in the fly-tying instructions to see how the hook is placed in vise.) If the hook sags, adjust the tightness of the vise a bit. However . . .

▸ **Be mindful of how tight you set the vise.** Do not overtighten the vise. If you do there will be a slight build-up of concentrated heat because of the compression that's produced when the jaws squeeze the metal of the hook. Especially on smaller hooks, the heat build-up could modify the temper in the hook and make it brittle. Believe me, you don't want to have a hook break just as you're about to land a big fish.

Let's Tie Some Flies

Here you'll learn how to tie four different and very effective flies: a streamer (Woolly Bugger), a dry fly (Black Gnat Parachute), an emerger

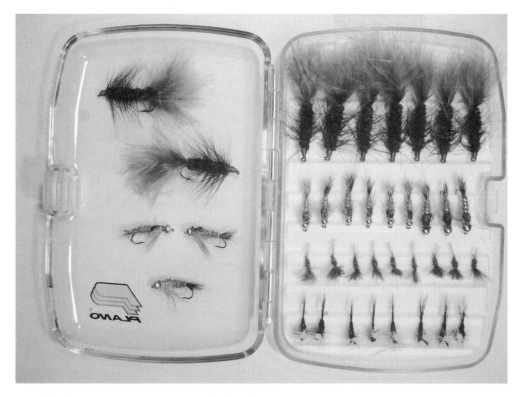

This fly box contains examples of the flies you will tie in this chapter (right side, top to bottom: Woolly Bugger, Bead-Headed Golden Ribbed Hare's Mask Nymph, CDC Emerger, and Black Gnat Parachute).

(CDC Emerger), and a nymph (Bead Headed Golden Ribbed Hare's Mask Nymph). These are my "go-to" flies; when I really want to catch a fish, these are the ones I'll likely use. As you tie each one, you'll learn basic skills that will apply to every other fly you'll ever tie. Also, as you read and learn more about fly tying, you'll learn additional skills and shortcuts and ways to work with different materials. Flytiers are creative artists, and you're now about to join their ranks!

Many of the techniques you'll learn in the steps that follow will require practice. Be patient with yourself as you start out. The more time you spend, the better you'll tie flies *and* catch fish.

WOOLLY BUGGER

The Woolly Bugger is arguably the most effective fly ever designed. Fortunately, it's also easy to tie. This fly and its close cousin, the Woolly Worm, embody many of the skills needed to tie more complex patterns, so they provide a great place to start. Also, since they're marvelously effective, you have an enhanced likelihood of early fishing success, which should evoke an increased desire to learn and tie more patterns.

Materials

Woolly Bugger.

Hook: Eagle Claw L058U, TMC 5263, or equivalent, size 6

Thread: Red or black, 6/0

Tail: Olive Marabou

Weight: Gudebrod's lead-free body wrap or other environmentally friendly wire, .015″–.030″, or thin-gauge soft lead electrical solder

Body: Olive, black, or teal chenille (about ⅛-inch diameter), 6 inches

Hackle: Black feather, 6 inches

Step 1. With the thread end in one hand and the bobbin in your dominant hand, cross the thread in front of the hook shank to form an X (see photo A). Hold the thread end firmly while you make a few wraps around the middle of hook shank with the bobbin as follows: Pass the thread over the shank and away from you, bring it down behind the shank, and finally toward you as the thread passes underneath the shank. After several overlapping wraps, allow the bobbin to hang while you raise the end of the thread straight up and cut it off just above and close to the hook shank.

Step 2. Wind the thread around the hook shank so that each turn of thread is right next to the last one (not on top of it). Wrap toward the hook bend. When you reach a point just before the hook bends, form a small bump of thread, which I call the *origin*, by winding eight or more times in the same spot (B).

Step 3. From the marabou feather, strip about $\frac{1}{2}$ inch of the soft feather material from the main shaft (B). You'll use this to make the tail. While holding the material tightly, compress it into a tight bunch by passing it back and forth between the thumb and index fingers of each hand.

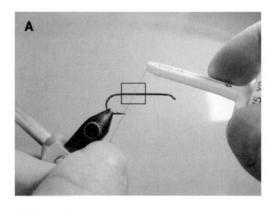

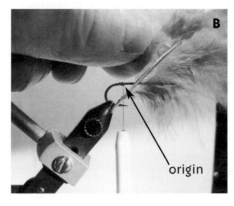

Make an X.

Form a bump of thread and tear off about $\frac{1}{2}$" of soft marabou feather material.

Step 4. Hold the bunch tightly in your dominant hand and place it along the top of the hook shank, with the tips pointing toward the hook bend, to measure the tail. The tail should be no longer than the total length of the hook. You can make small adjustments in the length by changing the pinch point to make it longer or shorter as you move the bunch back and forth between your hands.

Step 5. Grasp the tail tightly between the thumb and index finger of the hand that's not holding the bobbin. Lay the base of the tail on top of the hook shank. To tie the tail you'll use the *critical pinch technique,* which allows you to tie it on top of the hook shank. To perform the critical pinch technique, you simultaneously pinch the hook shank and the tail fibers

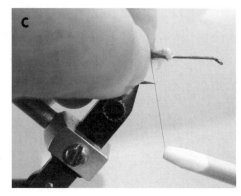

Use critical pinch technique to tie tail on top of hook shank.

and firmly wrapping the thread while ensuring that the material does not roll around the shank. Wrap the thread firmly with three or more full turns before letting go. This technique may take some practice, but it is essential that you learn it. To tie the Woolly Bugger's tail, you'll first shorten the length of thread extending between the bobbin and the hook shank to about 1 or 2 inches, which will both give you room to work and limit the chances of breaking the thread as you wrap it. While maintaining your pinch on the tail against the top of the hook shank, do the following: Draw the thread upward, so it passes under your thumb. Now you're pinching both the thread and the tail. Pass the thread over the tail, and then draw the thread straight down on the back side of the hook (C).

Before tightening the first loop, pass the thread beneath the hook and back toward you, and make another loop the same way as before. Then bring the bobbin straight down on the back side of the hook to carefully but firmly tighten the loops. Before letting go of your pinch, make at least three more firm turns of thread to secure the tail to the top side of the hook shank.

It's critical to tie the marabou on top of the hook shank and not have it roll around the shank, as it's likely to do if you hold the clump limply or wrap the thread too loosely.

Cut off the excess marabou butts and residual pieces of the feather's shaft about ¼ inch beyond the origin. Then make several more tight turns of thread to really bind in the material.

If the tail looks too thin, strip another ½ inch of feathery material and repeat the critical pinch technique. If necessary, repeat this process until you're satisfied that fish will want to chase that tail. If the tail is longer than the overall hook (in which case fish will bite the tail and not get hooked) or shorter than it (in which case the tail won't undulate as well), gently pull the appropriate end of the marabou bunch to adjust the length.

Step 6. The Woolly Bugger is a wet fly, so it needs extra weight to sink. Make ten or more tight, side-by-side wraps of soft metal wire around the hook (D), starting right next to the marabou butts and working toward the hook eye. Stop at least ⅛ inch before the eye. With the base of the scissor blades, break or cut off the excess wire.

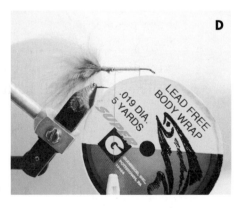

Wrap wire around hook shank.

To help hold the wire coil in place, cover it with turns of thread. Wrap the thread back and forth a couple of times along the length of the coil, leaving enough space just behind the hook eye to finish the fly later. End your last thread wrap at the origin.

Step 7. Hold the hackle by the tip. With your other hand, gently stroke the feather downward until the individual bristles are more perpendicular to the feather shaft (E). Place the hackle tip at the origin so it points toward the hook eye. Use the critical pinch technique to tie in the tip (F), covering about ½ inch or less of the tip. For now, the body of the feather will extend beyond the tail until it's time to wrap the hackle.

Step 8. At the origin, tie in the chenille (F), allowing about 1 inch of excess to extend toward the hook eye and its length to extend back with the long feather. Wrap the thread forward to just behind the eye while tying in that extra inch of chenille. Now let the bobbin hang. You'll use the thread to secure the chenille and hackle after each is wrapped forward.

Stroke out bristles from long hackle feather.

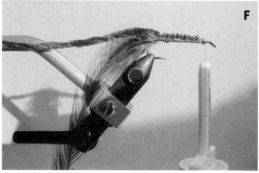

Tie tip of hackle and then tie chenille onto top of hook shank.

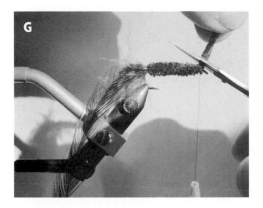

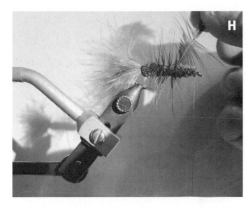

Wrap chennile tightly forward to just behind hook eye.

Palmer or wrap the hackle feather forward to just behind eye.

Step 9. To create the body, make tight, side-by-side wraps of chenille to about ⅛ inch behind the hook eye (G). The wraps should be right next to each other to make a fuzzy body. When the body has been formed, wrap at least three turns of thread over the chenille to capture the tag end in place. Then hold the tag end of the chenille straight up and cut it close to the eye. Be careful not to cut the thread.

Step 10. With the butt end in hand, wrap the hackle forward toward the hook eye (H). This process is called *palmering*. Evenly space each turn about ⅛ inch apart, or about the width of the chenille. When the butt end of the feather reaches just behind the hook eye, secure it there with three or more turns of thread, making sure you tie in the stem of the feather. Then hold the excess part of the feather straight up and cut the stem with the middle of the scissor blades.

Step 11. To finish the head, tie about six half hitches. To make a half hitch, draw off a couple of inches of thread from the bobbin. Lay the tapered end of a BIC pen casing on the thread so the thread forms

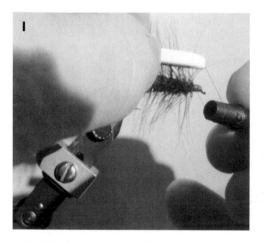

To tie a half hitch, make a U in thread.

Twist half hitch tool and drop half hitch over hook eye.

a U around the casing (I). Then make one twist in the U, place the hole of the casing directly over the hook eye, and drop the half hitch just behind the eye (J). Repeat until you have a total of six half hitches.

Step 12. Cut the thread when you're finished making the head. With a bodkin, apply a small drop of fly-tying cement or clear fingernail polish to glue the thread in place (K). Avoid getting the glue in the hook eye. If glue does get into the eye, pass a small feather tip, butt first, through the eye to clear it out.

After cutting thread, finish fly by applying a dab of cement.

Congratulations! You have just completed your first fly, and you're well on your way to becoming a flytier. Don't fret if your fly doesn't quite match a store-bought fly. Keep practicing this recipe, and soon you'll be tying great Woolly Buggers.

BLACK GNAT PARACHUTE

I have caught more fish in more locations with a Black Gnat Parachute than any other dry fly. It's so successful that my fishing buddy suggests that the military put one in every survival kit.

As the name suggests, parachute flies always land upright on the water. These flies have a post of tightly wound hair fibers located on top of the hook shank about one-third to one-quarter down the length of the shank from the eye. The post, which holds the "parachute," helps you spot your fly more easily—you can modify the color of the post to increase the fly's visibility. Ultimately, you want a post that's light and will not hold water.

Materials

Hook: TMC 100, Eagle Claw D059F, or Mustad 94840, size 12–18
Thread: Black, 6/0
Tail: Woodchuck tail guard hairs or long side-feather fibers of a black dry-fly hackle
Post: White caribou hair or polypropylene or other synthetic fiber
Abdomen: Super-fine dubbing (Umpqua)
Hackle: Black dry-fly feather (minimal webbing), $1/4$-inch side fibers

Black Gnat Parachute.

TIP: When a dry fly calls for feather fibers, avoid the fibers nearest the base of the feather, where there is considerable webbing. The webbing, visible under a magnifying glass, consists of small bristles on each fiber. When wet, these bristles hold water and can cause a dry fly to sink.

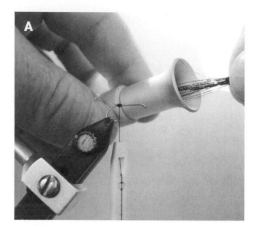

Use a hair stacker to align hair tips.

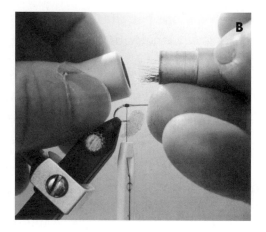

Draw away bottom of hair stacker to reach aligned hair tips.

Step 1. Place the hook securely in the vise and create an origin with your thread, just as you did for the Woolly Bugger. Cut a bunch of woodchuck tail hair (15–20 hairs) from the hide and place it in a hair stacker (see photo A), tips first. Turn the stacker upright and tap the bottom of it several times to align the tips. With the stacker in a horizontal position, carefully pull off the bottom. Grasp the hair tips firmly and remove the hair from the top part of the stacker (B).

Step 2. Place the bunch along the top of the hook shank so the tips extend one hook length beyond the hook bend. This is the tail. Use the critical pinch technique to tie in the tail at the origin. Shorten or lengthen the tail as needed by slowly pulling the bunch rearward or forward. For proper balance, the tail should be no longer than one hook length. If you're using woodchuck tail or other long hairs, do not cut the butt ends of the tail fibers at this time.

To secure the tail, wrap the thread tightly forward to about one-third shank length from the hook eye, and let the bobbin hang.

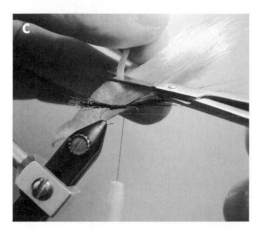

Clip close to hide 10–12 white caribou hair fibers.

Tie in the woodchuck tail fibers along with the caribou hair about $1/3$ back from the hook eye.

Step 3. Cut about 10 or 12 caribou hairs from the hide; cut as close to the hide as possible (C). Tie the hairs in where the bobbin hangs, wrapping the thread around the midpoint of the hairs.

Step 4. To make the post, integrate the woodchuck hair and the caribou hair (D). Hold the hair straight up and wrap the thread around the hook shank directly in front of its base (E).

Step 5. Starting where the upright hair meets the shank, wind the thread upward around the base. To avoid cutting the hollow caribou hairs with the thread, make your first few turns around

Make a few thread wraps in front of where the fibers meet the hook shank.

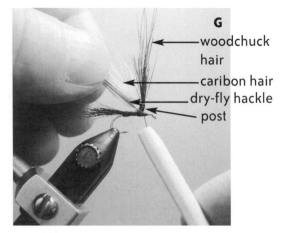

Firm up the post by wrapping the thread horizontally upward about ¹⁄₈ inch from the hook shank.

Tie dry fly hackle feather in at base of post.

the base somewhat loose, and then increase the tension as you work up the post.

Wrap the thread about ¹⁄₈ inch up the post (F). To stabilize the base, apply a small drop of head cement or clear fingernail polish with the bodkin.

Step 6. With the tip pointing upward, tie in the butt of the dry-fly hackle behind the hook eye and pointing back toward the post (G). Make horizontal wraps around the base of the post to finish tying in the hackle. (Note: Tie in only the part of the feather that has minimal or no webbing.)

Step 7. When the hackle is tied in, wrap the thread back down the post to the hook shank and make a wrap or two vertically just behind the post nearest the tail. Make a very thin dubbing rope (H) as follows: With the hand that's not holding the bobbin, take a small amount of super-fine dubbing and place it alongside the thread. Using your thumb and forefinger, twist in the same direction the dubbing and thread together to make a "rope" that's about double or triple the diameter of the thread alone. When making dubbing ropes, it's almost always best to have it as thin as possible. Repeat this process until you have about 3 inches of dubbed thread (I). Dubbing takes a bit of practice, so persist in trying to get the process perfected. Try putting lotion on your hands to give them

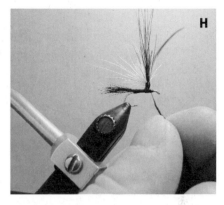

Twist dubbing on thread to make a very thin dubbing rope.

some moisture—which should make twisting easier—and always twist the dubbing material and thread in the same direction.

Step 8. Wrap a cigar-shaped abdomen with the dubbing rope. Start by wrapping non-dubbed thread to the origin, where you will make your first turns with the dubbing (J). Wrap the dubbing from the

Make about 3 inches if thin dubbing rope.

Beginning at the origin, wrap sparse dubbing rope forward to just ahead of the post.

origin toward the base of the post. *Note that if you make too many turns of dubbing near the origin, you'll add too much bulk in that section and not achieve the desired taper for the abdomen.* Make side-by-side turns until you reach the base of the post. Remove the dubbing material from the excess dubbed thread, and then make a few more turns with the clean thread just behind the post. Next, wrap the thread forward to just behind the hook eye, and let the bobbin hang.

Step 9. With the hackle pliers, pinch the tip of the hackle and wind it six to eight full turns horizontally around the post in a clockwise direction, making your last turn near the base of the post (K). The feather may be brittle, so be careful not to exert too much pressure as you wrap it around the post. Also be careful not to pull the feather out of the hackle pliers.

Step 10. Wrap the feather along the hook shank to the eye, and then allow the pliers to hang while you secure the tip to the hook

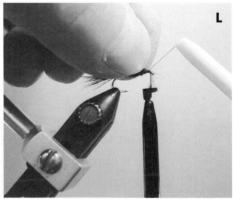

Use hackle pliers to wrap the dry fly hackle around post.

Capture the hackle tip by making at least three wraps binding it to the hook shank just behind the hook eye. Lightly pulling back on the post will provide just a bit more room to help capture the hackle tip.

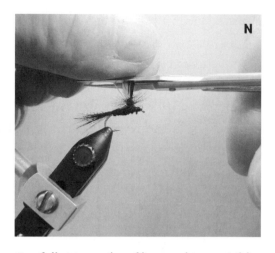

To secure the fly, use a tool to make half hitches.

Carefully trim caribou fibers making a visible 3/16 inch post.

shank with three or more wraps of thread just behind the hook eye. If you need more space to make your thread wraps behind the hook eye (L), carefully pinch back the post to give you a bit more room to work. Once the hackle is secure, raise any excess feather and carefully cut it away. Be careful to not cut the thread.

Step 11. Using the ink tube from a BIC pen, tie six half hitches (M). For extra durability, use a bodkin to place a small drop of fly-tying cement or clear nail polish on the knots. Finally, carefully trim the post to $3/16$ inch above the hackle "parachute" (N). Using the above technique, you can easily substitute black for gray dubbing and grizzly and brown hackle to make a Parachute Adams—another very effective dry fly.

CDC EMERGER

This fly is so simple to tie, you should be sure to tie several of various sizes or colors so you always have enough in your fly box.

Materials

Hook: Eagle Claw D057F, Mustad AC 3906, or
    Daiichi 1100, size 16–20
Thread: Olive or black, 6/0–8/0
Shuck or Tail: Antron carpet fiber (olive or
    tan) or a few fibers from old panty
    hose
Wing: 3–4 CDC feathers
Thorax: Hare's mask dubbing

CDC Emerger.

TIP: If you're using 8/0 thread, be very careful not to apply too much tension as
you wrap it. Also, a simple nick with the hook's tip might be enough to break
the thread. Be careful!

Step 1. Place the hook securely in the vise and create an origin with your
thread (see photo A). For the trailing shuck, tie in about 10 to
15 Antron fibers at the top of the hook shank at the origin (B).

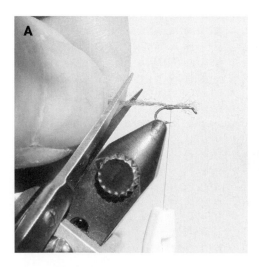

*Form an X with thread and hook shank
and make a bump of thread at hook bend.*

Tie in about 10–15 antron fibers.

They should not extend more than a hook shank's length beyond the hook bend. Remember, an emerger is crawling out of its shuck, so your shuck should be fairly sparse. When the fly is in the water, the Antron will just hint at a structure that will be mostly "filled" with water. Trim the Antron to the proper length, and then wind the thread forward to about one-third shank's length from the hook eye.

Step 2. For a wing, choose three or four CDC feathers and tie them in about one-third shank's length from the hook eye (C). Their length above the hook shank should be about the same as the shank length. For now it's OK if they overhang the eye.

Step 3. To achieve an upright position for the wing, pinch and hold the feathers upward and toward the rear of the fly while you wrap a few turns of thread just in front of them, between the base of the feathers and the hook eye (D).

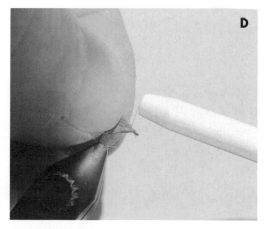

To create wings, tie in about 4 CDC feathers about ¹/₃ back from hook eye.

Wrap a few turns of thread between the feathers and the hook eye.

Twist a small amount of soft hare under fur to make a sparse dubbing rope.

Wrap dubbing rope forward from origin to base of wing.

Step 4. Twist a very small amount of hare's mask dubbing onto the fly-tying thread (E), and then wind the non-dubbed thread to the origin where you'll begin to wrap the dubbing. To create a cigar-shaped, tapered thorax, start wrapping the sparse dubbing rope up to where the CDC feathers are tied in (F). Avoid building up too much bulk in any one spot.

Step 5. Remove any excess dubbing you may have on the thread, and then wrap the thread a few turns ahead of the CDC feathers to just behind the hook eye. Use the ink tube of a BIC pen to tie four to six half hitches (G), and finish the head in the usual manner.

Use a tool to tie half hitches behind the hook eye.

BEAD-HEADED GOLDEN RIBBED HARE'S MASK NYMPH

Both the fly's name and its application are a mouthful. (I couldn't resist!) This is really a fantastic and effective fly. When the fish are not eating at the water's surface, they're eating below it, and this fly will get you to the feeding zone. Of the four flies we're tying, this is by far the most complex. It does, however, build upon some of the skills you've learned so far, and you'll learn a few additional tricks as well.

First, here's some information to keep in mind as we tie the nymph. All insects have three segments: head, thorax or mid section, and abdomen. We also know that insects have six legs, but since fish can't count, a few extra legs won't matter as long as the fly has something that looks like legs. The important goal here is to make a fly that's appealing to fish.

Materials

Hook: Mustad 3906B, Eagle Claw L058U, or
Daiichi 1710, size 8–12
Thread: Brown or black, 6/0
Head: Brass fly-tying bead, $^5/_{32}$ inch
Tail: Hare's mask guard hairs
Abdomen: Hare's mask underfur
Rib: Brass wire or gold braided tinsel, fine,
4 inches
Wing Case: Turkey, pheasant tail feather
fibers, or Gudebrod sinew wrap, tan
Thorax: Hare's mask plus or hare's mask
guard hairs
Legs: Mallard, green-wing teal, or wood
duck striated flank-feather fibers

Bead-Headed Golden Ribbed Hare's Mask Nymph.

Step 1. Look at the brass fly-tying bead. Notice that the hole on one side is smaller than the hole on the other side. Insert the hook point into the smaller hole, and slide the bead around the hook bend and down the shank to the hook eye. The bead both represents the

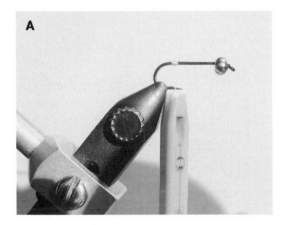

Insert hook point into small hole on bead and then form an origin bump by winding thread at hook bend.

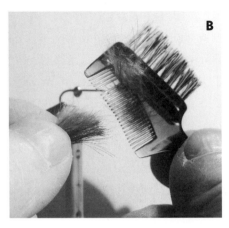

Cut a small clump of guard hairs from a hare's mask and comb out the soft underfur.

insect's head and adds weight to the fly, which will allow it to sink to where the fish are feeding.

Now place the hook securely in the vise and create an origin with your thread (see photo A).

Step 2. For the tail, cut a bunch of hare's mask hair as close to the hide as possible (B). Holding the bunch tightly between your thumb and forefinger, remove the soft underfur by combing the bunch with the smallest mustache or eyebrow comb you can find or a doll's comb. If you don't have such a comb, gently tease out the soft fur with your fingers. Set the collected underfur aside for use in step 5.

Step 3. Lay the butts of the guard hairs along the top of the hook and use the critical pinch technique (see page 210) to tie them in at the origin (C). Most of the hairs should extend no longer than a hook gap's distance—the vertical distance between the shank and the point of the hook—beyond the hook bend. Ideally you should have between forty and sixty guard hairs in the tail. If you think you need to tie in additional guard hairs, do so.

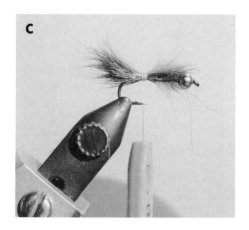

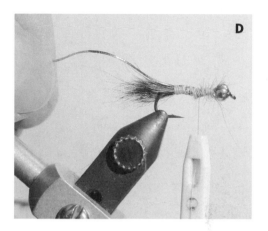

Tie the guard hairs onto the top of the hook shank.

Neatly wrap the guard hair butts then tie in a short length of braided gold tinsel.

When the tail is bulky enough, make a few extra wraps of thread to secure it firmly in place. Then wrap the thread back to the origin.

Step 4. Tie in the wire or tinsel (D) at the origin, and allow its length to extend beyond the hook bend until we wrap the rib. Wrap the thread around the tied-in ends of guard hairs and rib material, up to the bead and back again, to create a relatively neat surface on which you'll tie the rest of the fly.

Step 5. Twist the soft rabbit underfur onto about 3 inches of thread to create a thin dubbing rope. Wrap the thinnest part of your rope around the origin and continue making tight side-by-side wraps, creating a cigar-shaped abdomen, until you reach the approximate center of the hook shank (E). Note that the abdomen can't fill more than two-thirds of the available hook shank space. If necessary, you can add more dubbing to the thread to achieve the right abdomen shape. On the other hand, if you have dubbing rope leftover after you wrap the abdomen, remove the excess underfur.

Twist the soft underfur onto the thread to form a sparse dubbing rope. Wrap the dubbing forward to the middle of the hood shank.

Make 3–4 evenly spaced wraps with gold tinsel.

When the abdomen is complete, wrap several turns of clean thread just ahead of it, and let the bobbin hang.

Step 6. Wrap the rib material forward, over the top of your dubbed abdomen, in three to four equally spaced turns (F). Secure the tag end of the rib firmly with three or more turns of thread. Then, using the base of your scissors, cut the rib close to the hook shank. If you look closely at an actual bug, you'll see that its abdomen has multiple segments. By winding the wire or tinsel forward, you create the illusion that your fly has something similar to the natural insect. And that's just how a fish will view your fly.

At this point, relax and admire your work so far. You're more than half finished, and your nymph has a tail, a head, and a segmented abdomen. Not bad! The only things missing are a midsection and some legs.

The midsection of a natural nymph has a couple of parts: a wing case, underneath which the wings will develop, and the thorax itself. Making these on your fly may get a bit tricky, so stay with me.

Step 7. To start a wing case, clip about eight to ten fibers from a wild turkey's tail feather and tie these in, dull side up, immediately forward of the abdomen (G). The length of the fibers should extend beyond the hook bend. In a few minutes we will fold the fibers up and over the thorax to complete the wing case. To help keep the fibers from separating, some flytiers apply a thin coat of head cement to the dull side of the feather.

Tie in 8–10 fibers from a turkey tail feather.

Step 8. The thorax gives rise to the legs and has a lot of moving parts. To create this visually active area within the one-third hook-shank-length area we have left, we will use dubbing wax and guard hairs to make a dubbing rope that bristles (H). First, draw about 3 inches of thread from the bobbin and down from the hook shank. Apply a light coat of dubbing wax to this section of thread to make it sticky. (Lip balm or a glue stick will work in a pinch.) Next, lightly apply a sparse coat of Hare's mask plus or hare's mask guard hairs along the sticky thread.

Pull down about 3" of thread and rub it with dubbing wax. Now lightly apply some hare's mask guard hairs.

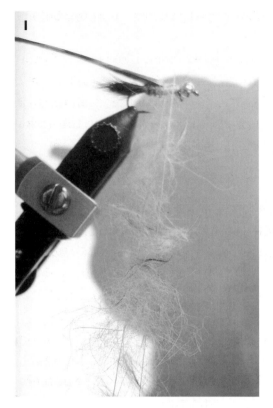

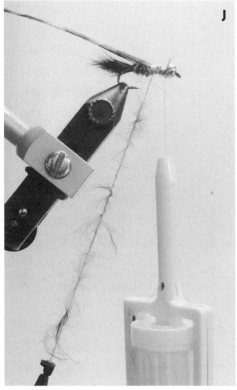

Holding down the dubbed side of the thread, form a thread loop back to the hook shank.

Grasp the bottom of the loop with a dubbing tool or hackle pliers and twist both strands until they come together in a dubbing rope that bristles.

Step 9. While holding the lower end of the coated thread straight down, draw off more thread from the bobbin, bringing the bobbin back to the shank, and make three or more turns of thread over the hook shank and near where the thread descends (I). You should now have a 3-inch loop hanging from the hook, with a lot of guard hairs stuck to the sticky thread side.

Step 10. With your hackle pliers, pinch the thread at the bottom of the loop. Allow the weight of the pliers to bring the two strands of thread together, and then spin the pliers gently to the right to twist the loop. By twisting the thread, the captured guard hairs will bristle outward. Make about thirty twists, but stop before the loop begins to kink up (J).

Alternatively, you can insert the two hook-like bends of your dubbing tool into the bottom part of the loop. Slowly and gently pull the loops together, capturing the hair fibers. Carefully spin the tool to create the dubbing rope. If you pull too hard, however, the hooks will pop from your loop and you might have to start over again.

Step 11. Wind the thread forward to just behind the bead, and let the bobbin hang. Then wrap the bristly dubbing rope forward in tight, side-by-side turns (K), just as you wrapped the chenille in the Woolly Bugger. Your last turn should be right behind the bead. Secure the dubbing rope with three turns of thread. Carefully clip off and discard the excess dubbing rope. Do not accidentally cut the bobbin thread!

Step 12. To complete the wing case, fold the tail fibers up and over the top of the thorax. The shiny side of these fibers should now be on top (L). Firmly hold the wing case while you secure it with three or more turns of thread right behind the bead. Once you're sure the wing case is secure, cut and discard the excess fibers.

Wrap the dubbing rope thickly just behind the bead and then capture the end by making three or more turns with the bobbin thread.

Fold over the turkey feather and tie it in just behind the bead.

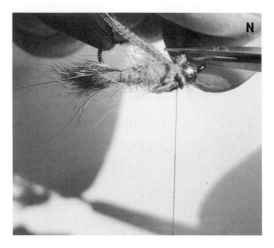

Invert the hook and tie in some variegated duck flank feather fibers to simulate insect legs.

Cut off the butt ends of the duck flank feathers close to the bead.

Step 13. To enable you to tie in a few legs, you need to take the fly out of the vise and invert the hook. If you have a rotary vise, you merely have to rotate the fly to expose the underside.

Grasp about 10 or 15 striated mallard, wood duck, or teal flank-feather fibers and cut them off near the feather shaft. Pinch the bunch and use the critical pinch method to tie it in with three or more turns of thread just behind the bead head (M). The fiber tips should extend toward the hook point. Cut off the excess butt ends close to where they were tied in (N).

Step 14. Find the part of a BIC pen that fits nicely over the bead head, and finish the fly with the usual half hitches (O). As you make each half hitch, let

Drop about six firm half hitches just behind the bead to secure the fly.

the knot slide off and rest just behind the bead. Use a bodkin to apply a small drop of fly-tying cement to the knots.

Time Check

Now you have completed the Bead-Headed Golden Ribbed Hare's Mask Nymph. I bet you can't wait to catch a fish with it!

This also marks the end of our time together. I'm sure you'll continue to use this book as a reference when you want to refresh your memory of a given skill. For example, if your casts aren't as good as you'd like, reread Hours 8–9, Casting with a Fly Rod and take a little time each day to practice the basics. Should you get tangles—as we all do—just sit down and set about the task of getting your line straightened out. There's no reason to stress about the situation. Remember, two big reasons why you're taking up this sport to begin with are to have fun and reduce stress. Take your time and be patient with yourself, especially while you're learning. Before you know it you'll be catching fish using guile and stealth with flies you tied. You won't ever forget the first time that happens. Did you save the world? Probably not. On the other hand, because you had a good day and a good experience fly-fishing, the many problems at hand were put into perspective. Just like the tangles in your fly line, you untangled those problems in a calm and methodical way.

From my perspective, there is absolutely nothing that compares to the sight of a fish taking my fly. That moment gives me a rush of adrenalin, and you can be sure I'm not thinking about much else. To be able to present a fly—your fly—to a living, breathing fish is quite an honor and a privilege. The manifestation of that honor comes when the fish takes your fly. . . . Whack! Fish on!

GLOSSARY

ANADROMOUS A type of fish that is born in fresh water and then goes out to sea, only to return to fresh water to spawn. Salmon and striped bass are typical examples.

ATTRACTOR PATTERN Often a very colorful or somewhat larger fly pattern that doesn't much look like any bug, fish, or food organism common to the area being fished. An attractor pattern usually looks so different from what the predator fish is familiar with that the pattern can induce a strike if nothing more than from curiosity.

BODKIN A small needle-like tool used for fly tying.

CDC Short for *Cul de Cunard*, CDC specifically refers to a specialized feather surrounding the oil gland of ducks and other water birds. CDC feathers hold the oil water birds use to preen their feathers, making them waterproof.

CRITICAL PINCH A technique flytiers use to tie in materials on the top of a hook shank, whereby the flytier pinches the material in place on the hook shank and uses a specific method of wrapping the thread to tie in the material.

CURRENT PLUME The expanding flow of water that exits a river and enters an embayment.

DOUBLE HAUL A technique used to add line speed during back- and forecasts. Two short strips are made with the noncasting hand: the first strip is executed as the fly line moves to the rear of the angler, and the second strip is executed just as the fly line begins to move forward during the casting sequence.

DOUBLE TAPER A type of fly line that has identical tapers at each end, allowing the line to be reversed if one end becomes worn. The center, or running part, of a double-taper fly line has a uniform thickness, which is generally larger in diameter than the ends and equal to the heavier shooting part of a weight-forward line.

DRAG The mechanism built into a fly reel that applies tension to the fly line as it is being pulled from the reel. The best drags are adjustable and apply resistance smoothly and uniformly when a fish is making a run.

DRY FLY A fly that floats on or above the water's surface film.

DUBBING Fine natural or synthetic fibers that, when twisted onto the fly-tying thread, add thickness, color, or texture to the thread. The result is a dubbing rope, or brush, which is wrapped concentrically around the hook shank to make prey bodies.

EMERGER A partially floating fly that simulates an insect transitioning from an aquatic life-form to a flying adult.

ESCAPEMENT A term used to indicate the numbers of adult fish needed to sustain a fishery. Once this number is achieved, fishery managers may increase the allowable creel limit.

FALSE CAST A casting technique whereby an angler keeps the fly in the air throughout multiple forward and rearward casting sequences. If not overused, a false cast is an effective way to move the fly from all the way downstream to an upstream position. Also used to air-dry a dry fly.

HACKLE A feather used in fly tying that comes from a chicken that is specially bred for such feathers.

HAUL A casting technique employed when the noncasting hand pulls a short amount of fly line through the guides. The quick pull is timed to increase line speed as a way of making longer casts.

LINE CONTROL A technique used by anglers to maintain a tight line back to the fly, permitting the rapid setting of the hook upon a fish strike. Good line control also helps the angler feel a strike on a wet fly, negating the need for strike indicators.

LOADING The process of transferring energy from the angler's hand and/or the fly line to the rod. This process occurs as the rod bends during both the forward and rearward parts of the casting sequence.

MENDING The act of putting an upstream arc in your fly line just as it falls onto the water's surface, so as to delay unnatural drag on the fly as it floats downstream.

NYMPH The part of an aquatic insect's life cycle most often characterized by bottom dwelling or free swimming. Nymphs are a major part of many freshwater fish species' diet.

ORIGIN A small bump of thread ever-so-slightly forward of the hook bend, where many materials are initially tied.

PALMERING Making consecutive and concentric spiral wraps of a feather during the process of tying a fly.

PALMING The pressure applied to a reel's outer rim by the palm of the angler's free hand to add friction to the drag of the reel.

PFD A personal flotation device, approved by the U.S. Coast Guard, to be worn by an angler or boater as an aid to remaining afloat upon falling into deep water.

REDD The nest of a fish. The term was formerly applied to salmon but now used for all nesting fish.

ROLL CAST A basic casting technique used to initially get fly line to lie straight out in front of the angler, or to make a cast when there are obstructions behind the angler, making a rearward cast improbable.

RUNNING LINE The part of weight-forward fly line after the first thirty feet. While this rear section of line has a slick coating, it generally has a much smaller diameter than the first thirty feet of the line.

SHOOTING The process of casting additional lengths of running line by using the speed and weight of the first thirty feet of the line to carry the additional line forward.

SHOOTING HEAD A fly line taper characterized by a heavier and shorter weight-forward section followed by a well-coated, slick, and small-diameter running line. Used for distance casting or casting into strong wind.

SHUCK The outer shell of an aquatic insect nymph left behind as it changes into its adult form.

SINKING TIP A fly line taper characterized by a front section that's heavier than water. Manufacturers build additional weight into this section to cause lines to sink at variable rates, depending on specification. The running line section floats, making for easier casts than would be possible with full sink lines.

SINGLE HAUL A technique used to add line speed during the backcast. The angler makes a short downward strip with his noncasting hand as the fly line is lifted from the water and moves rearward during the casting sequence.

SNAP-STOP The abrupt and controlled stop of the fly rod tip at the 1 o'clock position during the backcast. The abrupt stop allows the energy in the rod to be transferred to the fly line as it unfurls rearward.

STANDING PART The main section of fishing line to which a knot is tied. See *tag end*.

STOPPER KNOT An overhand knot tied at the tag end of the fly line to prevent the main knot from slipping out.

STRIKE INDICATORS In nymph fishing, a yarn, foam tab, or dry fly attached to the upper part of the leader some distance from the sinking nymph pattern. Should a fish strike the nymph, the indicator is pulled, alerting the angler to strip-set the hook.

STRIP The pulling action of the noncasting hand used to retrieve fly line after casting.

STRIP SET The act of impaling the hook in the fish's mouth achieved by sharply retrieving fly line with the noncasting hand. The strip set is used with wet flies, including streamers.

STRIPPING BASKET A lightweight tub or basket attached around the waist of a fly angler to hold and control stripped fly line prior to making the next cast. It's most often used in fast-flowing or turbulent water.

STRIPPING GUIDE The first guide on the fly rod, located just above the cork handle.

STREAMER A type of wet fly that's tied to look like a swimming fish or leech.

TAG END The short piece of fishing line that remains after a knot is tied. This end is usually expendable and is generally cut off close to the knot.

TAILING A feeding posture often associated with marine shallow water, bottom-feeding fish, like bonefish, when their tails are above the water's surface as they forage for something to eat.

TAILING LOOP A faulty loop formed in a fly line when the rod tip does not follow a level or straight path during a forecast. What usually happens is the loaded rod tip dips below horizontal before springing back. This down-and-back concave path of the rod tip forms the loop, and the loop forms the so-called wind knot.

TAIL WATER A river or stream downstream of a dam. When viewed from above, the lake upstream of the dam looks like the body of an animal, and the thin stream blow the dam looks like the animal's tail.

TANDEM RIG Two flies tied onto an angler's line at the same time. The first fly is the *primary fly* and the second fly is called a *dropper*. When a dry fly is used as a primary fly, it also can serve as a strike indicator.

TAPERED LEADER The terminal part of a fly line, onto which a fly is tied, that is generally made of clear monofilament fishing line. Its thickest diameter is located where it connects to the fly line, and the diameter progressively decreases as it extends toward the fly.

TIPPET Fly line leader material that is used to extend the original leader to a desired length, taper, and breakage strength.

TIP SET The act of impaling the hook in a fish's mouth by sharply raising the rod tip. The noncasting hand merely holds the fly line from slipping. The tip set is used with dry flies.

TRADITIONAL CAST A complete cast, including both the rearward and forward casting sequences.

TURBIDITY The amount of sediment suspended in the water and its impact on water clarity.

WATER HAUL Using the friction of the fly line lying on the water in front of the angler to help load the rod during the rearward casting sequence.

WEBBING Small fibers located on each bristle of a feather. Webbing is most apparent at the base of a feather, and it decreases in amount as the bristles progress toward the tip.

WEIGHT-FORWARD A fly line taper where most of the weight is in the first thirty feet of the line.

WET FLY A sinking fly that is fished below the water's surface.

WET-WADE A method of wading in warm water, in which anglers wear only their shoes or special low-cut boots.

WIND KNOT An overhand knot caused by a tailing loop when the rod tip dips below the straight-line path during the forward casting sequence.

RESOURCES

Equipment Checklist

In the following equipment list I suggest a number of pieces you may want to consider when building your fly-fishing tackle. Hopefully, even if you know nothing about fishing, this checklist can help orient you to products that will enhance your fly-fishing experience. This is by no means a complete list. Not every angler will need every item listed and, without doubt, other long-time fly anglers will suggest additional or alternate items. If you have limited time to shop around, any of these items and brands will do the job very well. Further, while you may be able to buy many of these items online, make an effort to go to the nearest fly shop, where you can get personal service and actually see, try on, and feel each product prior to making the final purchase.

Freshwater Tackle

✔	ITEM	DESCRIPTION	SOURCE
	Fly rod	Medium flex, 5- or 6-weight	March Brown (seven-piece travel rod), Albright, Scientific Angler, Shakespeare (two-piece rods)
	Reel	Low Medium High	Pflueger (Medalist) Sth J. Austin Forbes
	Fly Line	WF6F	Scientific Angler, Cortland, Royal Wulff, Rio
	Backing	20 lb. test Dacron	Gudebrod, Cortland
	Tippet	4X, 5X, and 6X (in spools)	Seaguar (fluorocarbon), Scientific Angler
	Leader	4X, 5X, and 6X (three each)	Scientific Angler (L2L system), Seaguar
	Monofilament fishing line	30 to 40 lb. test (5 feet to make terminal loop on fly line); Maxima or Stren 8 or 10 lb. test (small spool to make leaders for practice); Stren (soft type)	

Saltwater Tackle

✔	ITEM	DESCRIPTION	SOURCE
	Fly rod	Medium flex, 8- or 9-weight	March Brown (multipiece for travel), Albright (two-piece rods)
	Reel	Pflueger (Trion), Sth (Cortland), J. Austin Forbes	
	Fly line	WF8F or WF9F	Scientific Angler, Cortland, Rio, Royal Wulff
	Backing	30 lb. test Dacron	Gudebrod, Cortland
	Tippet	2X, 0X, and 02X (in spools)	Seaguar (fluorocarbon), Scientific Angler
	Leader	2X, 0X, and 02X (3 each); 3- to 6-inch wire leader for fish with sharp teeth	Seaguar (fluorocarbon), Scientific Angler, Rio

Clothing and Accessories

✔	ITEM	DESCRIPTION	SOURCE
	Sunglasses	Bronze polarized	
	Chest waders	Stocking foot or boot foot	Hodgman, Dan Bailey, Albright
	Wading boots	Studded felt bottoms	Hodgman, Korkers
	Wading staff	Collapsible	Folstaf (w/compass), Fulcrum
	Landing net	Collapsible	Gudebrod
		Wood	Signature Concepts
	Hat	Broad brim w/chin strap	Ultimate, Tilley
	Clothing	Long sleeve shirts w/SPF rating	Ex Officio, Bug Off, Albright, Columbia
	Convertible pants	With zip off legs (convert to shorts)	Ex Officio, Albright, Columbia
	Fleece	Pullover	
	Wading pants	With ankle straps	L.L. Bean
	Fishing jacket	Multipocket	L.L. Bean, Bass Pro, Cabelas
	Chest pack	Use in lieu of fishing jacket	Orvis, William Joseph, Cabelas, Eagle Claw

Miscellaneous

✔	ITEM	DESCRIPTION	SOURCE
	Backpack	Lightweight, with side compression straps and water bottle pockets for holding travel rods	EMS, L.L. Bean
	Cement	Pliobond	
	Clippers	Fingernail clippers (small) or fly-fishing clipper with needle fishhook eye cleanout	
	First Aid Kit	Small	
	Fishing license	State fish and wildlife agency	Online, nearest tackle shop, Wal-Mart
	Flashlight	Gooseneck light	Zelco, Coast
	Flies	Variety of dry and wet flies	Cabelas, Bass Pro Shops, Orvis, L.L. Bean
	Floatant	Dry-fly	Scientific Angler, Loon
	Fly box	One for dry flies and one for wet flies	Plano, Millstream, Wheatley
	Fly-O	Practice fly rod	Royal Wulff
	Forceps (hemostats)	Assist in removing deeply Imbedded hooks	
	Knot-tying tool	Assists in tying four-twist loop and nail knot	Lake Products (knot-tying tool)
	Reel lubricant	Teflon grease, small tube	Super Lube
	Stripping basket	Collapsible	March Brown, Umpqua Feather Merchants
	Whistle	Use to signal someone in event of emergency	
	Zingers	Retractable cords to hold clippers, etc.	

Flies

Freshwater Flies

FLY NAME	SIZE
Adams	12, 14, 16
Ants	16
Bead-Headed Golden Ribbed Hare's Mask Nymph	12, 14, 16
Black Gnat Parachute	12, 14, 16
Blue-Wing Olive	16, 18, 22
CDC emergers	18, 20
Elk-Hair Caddis (Dark-Wing)	12, 14, 16
Elk-Hair Caddis (Tan-Wing)	12, 14, 16
Griffiths Gnat	18, 22
Hornberg	10, 12
Joe's Hopper	8
Pheasant-Tail Nymph	14, 16
Royal Wulff	14
Woolly Bugger (Black)	6, 8
Woolly Bugger (Olive)	6, 8
Woolly Bugger (Teal)	6, 8

Saltwater Flies

FLY NAME	SIZE
Clouser (Black)	2, 4, 6
Clouser (Chartreuse-and-White)	2, 4, 6
Crab	2, 4
Crazy Charlie	6, 8
Deceiver (Blue)	2/0
Deceiver (Chartreuse)	2/0
Deceiver (Gray)	2/0
Gotcha	6, 8

Fly-Fishing Equipment Manufacturers

Below is the contact information for many manufacturers of fly-fishing tackle, tools, materials, clothing, and so on. Following the contact info of each manufacturer is a list of the products the manufacturer carries. This is by no means a complete list. Although things can change over time, at the time of this writing, these manufacturers are known to be in business and carry the specific items included in the list. Mega sites like Bass Pro, Cabelas, and Gander Mountain also carry most items, but they offer little service online. Ideally you would be able to visit one of these stores. Otherwise, contact your nearest full-service fly shop and arrange to purchase most of your items there. You might also consider attending a fly-fishing consumer show when one comes to your area. Certainly, many of the largest vendors will be there, and you can test many of their products prior to purchasing.

Travel Rods

Albright Tackle, LLC
300 Jericho Quadrangle
Jericho, NY 11753
866/359-7335
www.albrighttackle.com

Cabelas
800/243-6626
www.cabelas.com

L.L. Bean
Main St.
Freeport, ME 04033
800/441-5713 (U.S./Can.)
www.llbean.com

March Brown
5 Anthony Ave.
Bristol, RI 02809
401/440-1001
www.marchbrown.com

Orvis
4200 Route 7A
Manchester, VT 05255
888/235-9763
www.orvis.com

Practice Fly Rod

Royal Wulff
7 Main Street
Box 948
Livingston Manor, NY 12758
800/328-3638
www.royalwulff.com

Fly Reels

J. Austin Forbes
www.jaustinforbes.com

Pflueger
www.pfleugerfishing.com

Shakespeare Fishing Tackle
3801 Westmore Drive
Columbia, SC 29223
800/334-9105
www.shakespeare-fishing.com

Sth
Cortland Line Co.
607/756-2851
www.cortlandline.com

Fly Line

Cortland Line Co.
607/756-2851
www.cortlandline.com

Rio Products International Inc.
5050 S. Yellowstone Highway
Idaho Falls, ID 83402
208/524-7760
www.rioproducts.com

Royal Wulff
7 Main Street
Box 948
Livingston Manor, NY 12758
800/328-3638
www.royalwulff.com

Scientific Anglers
3M Corporate Headquarters
3M Center
St. Paul, MN 55144
888/364-3577
www.scientificanglers.com

Backing

Cortland Line Co.
607/756-2851
www.cortlandline.com

Gudebrod
274 Shoemaker Rd.
Pottstown, PA 19464
877/249-2211
www.gudebrod.com

Leaders/Tippet

Climax
Cortland Line Co.
607/756-2851
www.cortlandline.com

Frog Hair
Gamma Technologies
200 Waterfront Drive
Pittsburgh, PA 15222
800/437-2971
www.froghairfishing.com

Scientific Anglers
3M Corporate Headquarters
3M Center
St. Paul, MN 55144
888/364-3577
www.scientificanglers.com

Seaguar/Grand Max
420 Lexington Ave.
New York, NY 10170
212/867-7040
www.seaguar.com

Mono Fishing Line

Maxima America
3211 S. Shannon St.
Santa Ana, CA 92704
714/850-5966
www.maxima-lines.com

Stren
Pure Fishing USA
1900 18th St.
Spirit Lake, IA 51360
800/237-5539
www.stren.com

Sunglasses

Action Optics
Smith Action Optics
P.O. Box 2999
280 Northwood Way
Ketchum, ID 83340
800/654-6428
www.actionoptics.com

Fisherman Eyewear
1700 Shelton Dr.
P.O. Box 261
Hollister, CA 95024
866/842-3474
www.fishermaneyewear.com

Chest Waders

Dan Bailey
P.O. Box 1019
209 W. Park St.
Livingston, MT 59047
800/356-4052
www.dan-bailey.com

Hodgman
Stearns Inc.
1100 Stearns Dr.
Sauk Rapids, MN 56379
800/333-1179
www.hodgman.com

Wading Shoes

Hodgman
www.hodgman.com

Korkers Products
1239 SE 12th Ave.
Portland, OR 97214
800/524-8899
www.korkers.com

Wading Staff

Folstaf
Fly Tyer's Carry All
112 Meade Rd.
Charlotteville, NY 12036
607/397-9133
www.folstaf.com

Fulcrum Sports Inc.
23 Carol St.
Clifton, NJ 07014
866/473-6900
www.fulcrumsports.com

Landing Net

Gudebrod
274 Shoemaker Rd.
Pottstown, PA 19464
877/249-2211
www.gudebrod.com

Signature Concepts
www.sigconcept.com

Hat

Tilley Endurables
3176 Abbott Rd., Building A
Orchard Park, NY 14127
800/363-8737
www.tilley.com

Ultimate Products Inc.
4897-C W. Waters Ave.
Tampa, FL 33634
800/477-4287
www.ultimatehat.com

Clothing

Albright Tackle, LLC
300 Jericho Quadrangle
Jericho, NY 11753
866/359-7335
www.albrighttackle.com

Ex Officio
Gateway North Corporate Park
3314 S. 116th St.
Tukwila, WA 98168
800/644-7303
www.exofficio.com

Sportif USA
1415 Grey St., Suite 101
Sparks, NV 89431
800/921-1655 (Aventura)
888/260-7676 (Waterfronts)
www.sportif.com

Fishing Vest

Bass Pro Shops
800/465-2628
www.basspro.com

L.L. Bean
www.llbean.com

Cabelas
www.cabelas.com

Chest Pack

William Joseph
800/269-1875
www.williamjosephfishing.com

Loon Outdoors
2728 S. Cole Rd., #110
Boise, ID 83709
208/362-4437
www.loonoutdoors.com

Orvis
www.orvis.com

Floatant

Loon Outdoors
2728 S. Cole Rd., #110
Boise, ID 83709
208/362-4437
www.loonoutdoors.com

Scientific Anglers
3M Corporate Headquarters
3M Center
St. Paul, MN 55144
888/364-3577
www.scientificanglers.com

Flash Light

Coast
www.coastcutlery.com

Petzl America
Freeport Center, M-7
P.O. Box 160447
Clearfield, UT 84016
801/926-1500
www.petzl.com

Princeton Tec
5198 Rte. 130
Bordentown, NJ 08505
609/298-9331
www.princetontec.com

Zelco
65 Haven Ave.
Mt. Vernon, NY 10553
800/431-2486
www.zelco.com

Fly Boxes

Millstream
www.millstreamproducts.com

Plano Tackle Systems
431 E. South St.
Plano, IL 60595
800/226-9868
www.planomolding.com

Wheatley
Angler Sport Group
6619 Oak Orchard Rd.
Elba, NY 14058
585/757-9958
www.anglersportgroup.com

Stripping Basket

March Brown Ltd.
5 Anthony Ave.
Bristol, RI 02809
401/440-1001
www.marchbrown.com

Umpqua Feather Merchants
P.O. Box 700
Glide, OR 97443
800/322-3218
www.umpqua.com

Fly Tab/Patch

Angler Sport Group
6619 Oak Orchard Rd.
Elba, NY 14058
585/757-9958
www.anglersportgroup.com

Millstream
www.millstreamproducts.com

Reel Lubricant

Cortland Line Co.
607/756-2851
www.cortlandline.com

Super Lube-Teflon
www.dupont.com

Zingers

Loon Outdoors
www.loonoutdoors.com

Orvis
www.orvis.com

Clippers

CVS
www.cvs.com

Orvis
www.orvis.com

Bass Pro Shops
800/465-2628
www.basspro.com

Forceps

Orvis
www.orvis.com

Bass Pro Shops
www.basspro.com

Knot Tying Tool

Koehler Industries
P.O. Box 265
Harland, MI 48353
800/632-5552
www.cinchtie.com

Lake Products Co.
P.O. Box 189
Capac, MI 48014
800-726-3501
www.knottying.com

Cement

Pliobond
Ashland Inc.
5200 Blazer Parkway
Dublin, OH 43017
614-790-3333
www.ashchem.com

Back Pack

EMS
Eastern Mountain Sports
1 Vose Farm Rd.
Peterborough, NH 03958
888/463-6367
www.ems.com

Sierra Trading Post
800/713-4534
www.sierratradingpost.com

Fly-Tying Supplies and Materials

Vises

Abel Quality Products
165 Aviador St.
Camarillo, CA 93010
805/484-8789
www.abelreels.com

Dyna-King Inc.
70 Industrial Dr.
Cloverdale, CA 95425
800/396-2546
www.dyna-king.com

Griffin Enterprises Inc.
465-A Ash Rd.
Kalispell, MT 59901
800/344-3150
www.griffinenterprisesinc.com

HMH
14 Maine St.
Box 18
Brunswick, ME 04011
207/729-5200
www.hmhvises.com

Regal Engineering
100 Prentiss St.
Orange, MA 01364
978/544-6571
www.regalvise.com

Renzetti Inc.
8800 Grissom Pkwy.
Titusville, FL 32780
321/267-7705
www.renzetti.com

Materials

Angler's Choice Fly Tying Materials
P.O. Box 828
Arco, ID 83213
208/527-2734
www.flytyingmaterials.com

Bass Pro Shops
www.basspro.com

Cabelas
www.cabelas.com

Feather Craft
www.feather-craft.com

The Hook & Hackle Co.
www.hookhack.com

Wapsi Fly Inc.
www.wapsifly.com

Hackle

Keough
www.hookhack.com

Metz
www.umpqua.com

Umpqua Feather Merchants
P.O. Box 700
Glide, OR 97443
800/322-3218
www.umpqua.com

Whiting
Line's End Inc.
291 Main St.
Marlborough, NH 03455
603/876-4944
www.linesend.com

Other Equipment Suppliers:

Dan Bailey, Full-service shop
P.O. Box 1019
209 W. Park St.
Livingston, MT 59047
800/356-4052
www.dan-bailey.com

Feather-Craft Fly Fishing, Full-service
shop
8307 Manchester Rd.
P.O. Box 19904
St. Louis, MO 63144
800/659-1707
www.feather-craft.com

The Fly Dealer Flies
Flydealer.com
P.O. Box 580786
Elk Grove, CA 95758
877/901-3597
www.flydealer.com

The Fly Shop, Full-service shop
4140 Churn Creek Rd.
Redding, CA 96002
800/669-3474
www.theflyshop.com

Bob Marriott's Flyfishing Store,
Full-service shop
2700 W. Orangethorpe Ave.
Fullerton, CA 92833
800/535-6633
www.bobmarriotts.net

The Mighty Fly Flies
8 Oak View Dr.
Aliso Viejo, CA 92656
949/233-4028
www.themightyfly.com

Stone River Outfitters LLC, Full-service
shop
132 Bedford Center Rd.
Bedford, NH 03110
603/472-3105
www.stoneriveroutfitters.com

West Marine
P.O. Box 50070
Watsonville, CA 95077
800/685-4838
www.westmarine.com

Camping Checklist

air horn

aluminum foil

backpack

batteries

binoculars

bug face net or bug jacket

camera w/extra batteries

camp shoes or hiking boots

canteen or water bottle

can opener (U.S. Military P38)

chest waders

clothes for 2–4 days

clothesline rope

coffee cup with lid

coffee pot

compass

cooking pot

cooking utensils

day pack or fanny pack

dishwashing soap

dry bag

duct tape

eyeglasses, spares

first-aid kit

flashlight or headlamp

fleece pants

fleece vest

flies, leaders (5X, 2X), tippet

fly rods (5-weight and 8-weight,
    spares)

fly reels

fly line (spare)

folding saw

fry pan

grill

GPS

hiking socks

hat

insect repellant

knife, hunting or fillet

Leatherman tool or Swiss Army knife

map

matches (waterproof)

mess kit w/utensils

plastic bags

polarized sunglasses

raincoat

sanitized hand wipes

sleeping bag (40°F)

sleeping pad

soap

stoves w/ fuel (2)

sunscreen (SPF 30)

tarp (8' x 10')

thermos

tent

toilet paper

towel

two-way radio

water filters (2)

waterproof sealant

ziplock bags

INDEX

Numbers in **bold** refer to pages with illustrations or tables.